Forward with Faith

Eagle Gate
Salt Lake City, Utah

Special appreciation is expressed to the contributors to this work for their willingness to share their thoughts and testimonies with youth. Each author accepts complete personal responsibility for the material contained within his or her chapter. There is no endorsement for this work (real or implied) by The Church of Jesus Christ of Latter-day Saints, the Church Educational System, or Brigham Young University.

Library of Congress Catalog Card Number:

Forward with faith / Especially for Youth, 2000

p. cm.

ISBN 1-57345-781-7 (pbk.)

1. Mormon youth—Religious life—Congresses. 2. Church of Jesus Christ of Latter-day Saints—Doctrines—Congresses. I. Especially for Youth (Program)

BX8643.Y6F67 2000

248.8'3—dc21 00-027026

Printed in the United States of America

10 9 8 7 6 5 4 3 2 1 72082 - 6668

CONTENTS

1

FORWARD WITH FAITH

Ronald Bartholomew

What does it mean to go "forward with faith"? Colossians 1:23 tells us: "If ye continue in the faith grounded and settled, and be not moved away from the hope of the gospel, which ye have heard, and which was preached to every creature which is under heaven; whereof I . . . am made a minister."

In this scripture there is a key to developing our own faith and helping others develop their faith also. An example of how this process works can be taken from the life of the apostle Peter, who continued in his faith through trials, temptations, and sorrow until he was first "grounded" and then "settled." Over time, his faith became so strong that he could not be "moved away from the hope of the gospel," which he had heard, no matter what happened to him. Eventually he became "a minister" through which the gospel was "preached to every creature which is under heaven." Wouldn't you like to develop faith such as that? Let's take a look at how this process worked in Peter's life, as well as how some latter-day youth have applied these principles in their lives.

Peter's faith became "grounded" the same way our faith becomes "grounded" today. Someone who had already discovered Jesus and his teachings introduced Peter to them. Then, by study and practice, he was able to obtain a sure witness or testimony from the Holy Ghost for himself. Peter's brother Andrew first discovered Jesus through the testimony of John the Baptist. Andrew immediately "followed Jesus," and after spending an entire day observing Christ and his teachings he was convinced that Jesus was the promised Messiah. Andrew then went immediately to his brother Peter and exclaimed, "We have found the Messias . . . the Christ," and he took Peter "to Jesus." Peter also became convinced that Jesus was the Son of God and when invited to follow Him, Peter "straightway left all, and followed Jesus" (JST John 1:36–42).

Why would a responsible adult such as Peter—a man with family and business responsibilities—leave everything to follow a perfect stranger? His faith must have been grounded in something of substance. At first, Peter went to see Jesus because of the testimony of his brother, but when, a few months later, Jesus pointedly asked Peter, "Whom say ye that I am?" Peter's emphatic response was, "Thou are the Christ, the Son of the living God." Jesus knew Peter's faith had not come from the many miracles he had seen Jesus perform nor the testimony of other men. The Savior explained: "Flesh and blood [human knowledge and experience] hath not revealed it unto thee, but my Father which is in heaven" (Matthew 16:15–17). Peter's faith in Christ was "grounded" because he had received a witness from the Holy Ghost.

Many of us obtain our testimony the same way. We learn and follow at the invitation of another, and in the process, become "grounded" in our faith as a result of a witness of the Spirit. I have seen this process work in the lives of many young people I have known.

In seminary one day my students and I were studying D&C 25:12, which reads: "For my soul delighteth in the song of the heart; yea, the song of the righteous is a prayer unto me, and it shall be answered with a blessing upon their heads."

A young man raised his hand and asked, "Does that

mean that if the music I listen to isn't a 'prayer to God' that it's bad?"

He and the four other young men sitting by him were members of the varsity football team at our school. It occurred to me that their opinions would be of interest to the other members of the class. After some discussion, we read this statement by Elder Boyd K. Packer of the Quorum of the Twelve Apostles:

"I would recommend that you go through your [tapes and CDs] and set aside those . . . that promote the so-called new morality, the drug, or the hard rock culture. Such music ought not to belong to young people concerned about spiritual development. Why not go through your collection? Get rid of the worst of it. Keep just the best of it. Be selective in what you consume and what you produce. It becomes a part of you" (*Ensign,* Jan. 1974, 28).

I didn't realize the impact Elder Packer's words would have on these five young men. When they came to class the next day, they brought a broom, a dustpan, a sledgehammer, a shoe box, and a large brown grocery bag. One of them raised his hand and said, "Brother Bartholomew, do you care if we go outside for a little demonstration?"

Wondering what they had in mind, I followed them outside with the rest of the class. I wasn't sure what they were going to do with the sledgehammer, so I looked on from a distance. They unloaded the grocery bag, which was full of tapes and CDs, and proceeded to smash them to bits with the sledgehammer.

One of the girls in the class exclaimed, "They're crazy! They could have traded them in for money!" One of the five young men overheard her and retorted "If they aren't good for us, they aren't good for anyone else either!"

After the demolition, they swept the pieces into the shoe box and presented it to me. I put the box on display in my classroom. News of the CD/tape smashing spread quickly through the school. Other boxes of smashed tapes and CDs began to appear as some other young people were "pierced in their hearts" and followed the example of these young men.

Their influence spread to other places as well. That summer I spoke at a youth conference in Show Low, Arizona, where I shared the story of these young men and even showed the box of smashed CDs and tapes. Early the next morning, before the meetings began, several excited youth and their leaders came into the chapel and exclaimed, "Brother Bartholomew! You've got to see this! Hurry! Come outside right now!"

When I got outside, I saw a group of youth gathered to play a game of baseball—with CDs! One of the young men had gone through his CD collection the night before and decided it was time for him to "straightway" leave it "all, and [follow] Jesus."

He had gathered his friends that morning for the great game. He was pitching, and his friends were taking turns at bat, sending CDs flying!

He later said he had already been challenged by his mother, his bishop, and a young woman he was interested in, to go through his CD collection and get rid of the worst of it. The example of the five young men in my seminary class and the prompting of the Spirit had given him the extra courage and motivation he need to finally go through with it.

At the conclusion of their game, they swept up what amounted to over $800 worth of inappropriate and unworthy CDs. They put the pieces in a box, and I took it with me to Flagstaff, Arizona, for another session of EFY the next week.

When I got there, I met a group of young men from Mesa, Arizona, who had both extreme hairstyles and dynamic personalities. Because of their charisma and enthusiasm, they were the life of the party that week. After hearing the stories of what those other young men had done, they came up to see the contents of the two boxes. The Spirit touched their hearts, and they knew what they had to do. Later that summer, they drove to another youth conference I was speaking at in Arizona to give me a bag of *their* broken CDs.

Just as Peter had been, each of these young people was brought closer to the Savior by the example and testimony of another. Then, prompted by the Spirit, they moved forward with faith to "leave all" and follow Him.

I had wondered if their faith was being "grounded" by the spiritual witness of truth, or if they had possibly just been caught up in the emotion of the moment or had even done what they did to call attention to themselves. As time passed, however, I learned that, like Peter's, their conversions had been genuine.

After summer came to a close and a new school year began, I was working at the seminary one day after school when four young men dressed in full missionary attire walked into my classroom. I didn't recognize them at first glance, but quickly realized they were the football players from my seminary class who had smashed their tapes and CDs almost a year earlier. They had stopped by the seminary to visit on their way home from the temple. All four had received mission calls and were preparing to enter the Missionary Training Center. I was happy to report to them how their example had influenced other young men to change their lives and more closely follow the Savior.

I learned that the young man from Show Low, who gave up $800 worth of CDs, was preparing to serve the Lord in the mission field. And the young men whom I had met at EFY in Flagstaff sent me a picture of them posing together—at the airport! They, too, had decided to straightway leave all for a great cause—full-time missions—and follow Jesus.

These are just a few examples of many Latter-day Saint youth who have heard the Lord's call through the words of another, felt the Spirit confirm that the principle was true, then moved forward with faith to follow Jesus.

The Savior said "If any man *will do [God's] will,* he shall *know*" (John 7:17; emphasis added). Our faith cannot become "grounded" in Christ unless we are willing to give up the things of the world and "straightway" follow him. Is there someone whose faith could benefit from your righteous example? Is there something in your own life that you could leave behind to more closely follow the Savior and have your own faith more perfectly "grounded"?

Once our faith has become "grounded" in a personal testimony, we need to "continue in the faith" until we are "settled" (see Colossians 1:23).

Elder Neal A. Maxwell has explained what it means to be "settled": "Being settled . . . is not the result of a single, sudden act. . . . It is like the pounding of one's pitons into the rocky and ascending surface of the windswept and sun-scorched straight and narrow path. Because one's pitons are [grounded], he can inch forward. . . . When one is so anchored, he can then avoid . . . falling away" (*We Will Prove Them Herewith* [1982], 18).

Peter's faith was "grounded" in a testimony that Jesus is the Christ, but he had to go through many settling experiences before he would have faith strong enough to trust *completely* in the Lord's power and words. Most of us believe Jesus is the Christ, but is our faith "settled" enough to believe his words without question and rely on his power completely? For Peter, developing this kind of faith required time, experience, and even practice.

For example, when Jesus invited Peter to come out of the ship and walk on the water, Peter did so, but "when he saw the wind" and the waves, "he was afraid" and began "to sink." The Lord reached out to Peter, as he does to us, and said, "O thou of little faith, wherefore didst thou doubt?" (Matthew 14:29–31).

At another time, Jesus was prophesying concerning the suffering and crucifixion he would undergo. Peter did not want to believe this could happen to Jesus. He said, "Be it far from thee, Lord: this shall not be unto thee." Jesus helped him understand that he needed to believe *all* his words. He reprimanded Peter, saying, "Thou are an offense unto me" (Matthew 16:21–23).

Later, when Jesus was washing the disciples' feet, Peter refused him, saying, "Thou shalt never wash my feet." Jesus corrected Peter again, saying, "If I wash thee not, thou hast no part with me" (John 13:5–8). That same evening, Peter boldly offered to lay down his life for the Lord, prompting Jesus to prophesy: "The cock shall not crow this day, before that thou shalt thrice deny that thou knowest me" (Luke 22:33). When the Savior's prophecy was fulfilled, Peter remembered the word of the Lord and "went out and wept bitterly" (Luke 22:61–62).

After his resurrection, the Lord appeared to the apostles and commanded them to take the gospel to the entire world. Apparently misunderstanding his call, Peter returned to his fishing business. The Savior came to him again, and said, "Lovest thou me more than these [the fish]?" Peter answered, "Lord, thou knowest all things; thou knowest that I love thee." Jesus helped Peter understand by instructing him: "Feed my sheep" (John 21:15–17).

Through these experiences Peter learned to completely trust in the Lord, his words, and his power. He emerged from these settling experiences to become "one of the greatest of men" (Bible Dictionary, s. v. Peter, 749). He found out for himself that the Lord would not give up on him but would continue to work with him until his faith was completely "settled."

It is my testimony that the Lord will do the same for all of us, if we will try to move forward with faith and strive to overcome our weaknesses. I saw this happen while working with a student during a Book of Mormon year in seminary. I had never met Angie before. It was the first day of school, and I was bearing my testimony of the power of reading daily from the pages of the Book of Mormon. All of a sudden Angie stood up, pointed her finger at me, and said: "I'm sick and tired of people telling me to read the Book of Mormon! It's boring, and I can't understand it!"

The entire class stared at her in disbelief, and as she realized what she had done, her face turned completely red. I had never experienced an emotional outburst of this type in any class. In an instant, all eyes went from her to me; and the looks on the faces of the students seemed to be saying, "Whatcha gonna do now, Brother Bartholomew?" I was speechless.

At the end of class, while the rest of the students were filing out, Angie cautiously approached me.

"I'm sorry, Brother Bartholomew. I don't know what came over me," she sheepishly explained. "I believe in the Church, and I believe in the scriptures. I have tried to read them before, I really have, but they just don't make sense to me. What can I do?"

I reached for a candy bar in my desk drawer. I asked Angie if she liked Baby Ruths.

"It's my favorite," she said. "Why do you ask?"

"Will you try reading 1 Nephi chapters 1–7 just one more time?" I asked, holding out the candy bar.

"Okay . . . You've got a deal," she said.

The next Monday morning before class we met to discuss what she had read.

"I have to admit, that story is pretty cool," she said. "Swords, cutting off heads, stealing plates—it was awesome!"

I could tell we had some work to do. For another candy bar, she agreed to continue reading for another week. After a few weeks she was enjoying the Book of Mormon enough that she was reading without the candy bar incentives.

When she got to 2 Nephi chapter 12, I remembered Elder Boyd K. Packer's suggestion that first-time readers skip the Isaiah chapters and come back to them later in order to keep momentum and finish reading the book (*Things of My Soul,* videocassette, 1993). I didn't want anything to get in the way of Angie's progress, so I suggested this to her and she agreed. I was pretty sure she would be able to continue without difficulty from there.

I was at home that next Saturday morning working around the house, when all of a sudden I realized I had forgotten to warn Angie about the longest and perhaps the most difficult chapter in the Book of Mormon—the allegory of the olive tree in Jacob chapter 5! I spent the rest of the weekend worrying that she would get there before I could "warn" her about it Monday morning.

Well, Monday morning came, and we met as usual to discuss the previous week's reading. As she entered my classroom, I could tell something was wrong. She had been crying—her eyes were red and swollen. *Oh no,* I thought, *she got there before I could tell her not to read it! Had it been that bad?*

What happened next was a surprisingly sweet experience for me as well as her. I want you to read what she said to me in her own words. (I had her record her experience after she shared it with me in person.)

"I'm so thankful for the Book of Mormon," she choked through her tears. "I found the answer to what I have been praying for in Jacob chapter 5!"

I thought, *What, are you . . . a gardener?* With all the talk in that chapter about digging, pruning, dunging, etc., I couldn't imagine out what question she had found an answer to!

She continued: "You know I've got a boyfriend."

Oh, I knew. She had told me about him. Even though she wasn't yet old enough to date, he had taken a serious liking to her. Unfortunately, he didn't have a good reputation with girls, and to make matters worse, he was older, he had a car, and in her words, he didn't "believe the things we do."

"I like him a lot," she said, "but being Mormon and all, I've set some pretty high goals for myself. I've been confused and upset, and I've prayed every night about what to do. The only answer I got was, 'Read your scriptures.' I kept thinking to myself, *How in the world is that going to help me? There's nothing in there about relationships with boys—just stories about the Church.* The more I read, the more confused I became.

"Then I got to Jacob chapter 5," she said. "In that chapter it says the Lord sees the bad fruit growing on the tree, and instead of just throwing the tree in the fire, he cuts off the branch that's bad and puts it in a corner of the garden where it can grow good fruit.

"To me this means instead of just throwing him away and dumping him and lying about why I am, I'll let him go (or cut him off) by telling him it's not right, I'm only fifteen years old, and I have three years of high school ahead of me. By letting him go, I'll let him grow. But if I keep him to myself, the branch (or my boyfriend) will get out of control and tangle me all up, and I'll never get out."

I was stunned. I thought, *How did you get all that out of Jacob chapter 5?* Then it was as if I could hear Nephi saying, "For I did liken all scriptures unto us, that it might be for our profit and learning" (1 Nephi 19:23). Angie had done that, by the power of the Holy Ghost.

I thought of this observation made by Elder Dallin H. Oaks of the Quorum of the Twelve Apostles: "When we read the scriptures we invite and make ourselves accessible to the communications of the Holy Ghost. . . . As a result, *the reading of the scriptures . . . [puts] us in a position where we can obtain inspiration to answer any . . . personal question, whether or not that question directly concerns the subject we are studying in the scriptures.*"("Studying the Scriptures," an address given to the seminaries of Salt Lake and Davis County Thanksgiving Devotional, Salt Lake Tabernacle, Nov. 24, 1985, 19–20; emphasis added).

I also remembered the promise made to the Church by President Ezra Taft Benson. He said: "There is a power [in the Book of Mormon] which will begin to flow into your lives the moment you begin a serious study of the book. You will find greater power to resist temptation. You will find the power to avoid deception. You will find the power to stay on the strait and narrow path" (in Conference Report, Oct. 1986, 6).

With the help of the Holy Ghost, Angie had received her answer in one of the most unlikely and difficult chapters in the Book of Mormon.

She continued: "I called my boyfriend on the phone,

invited him over, and read the entire chapter to him. He was confused at first, but then I explained to him that I was breaking up with him—to help us both."

She had done what Peter and so many others down through the ages have done—amidst the traps of discouragement, misunderstanding, and mistakes, she continued to move forward with her faith until she received sufficient strength from the Lord to overcome her problem. Angie's faith was becoming more "settled."

I bear testimony that as you continue to move forward in faith through the challenges and temptations of your life, you too will experience the sustaining help of the Lord. And, like Peter and Angie, your faith in Him will become increasingly more "settled."

Once he became "grounded and settled," Peter was one who could not be "moved away from a hope of the gospel." He became a powerful minister who made it possible for the gospel to be "preached to every creature which is under heaven." He testified boldly of Christ in Jerusalem, continually standing up against the political and religious enemies of the newly formed Church. He was beaten and imprisoned by the same people responsible for the death of Christ. As president of Christ's Church, he dealt daily with the problems and growing pains associated with assimilating new converts from diverse backgrounds. Peter's faith eventually became so strong that the humble followers of Christ "brought their sick into the streets, . . . that . . . the shadow of Peter passing by" might heal them (Acts 5:15).

Once we become "grounded and settled" in our faith, we will be anxious to bless the lives of those around us. Like Peter, we will want to take the message of the gospel, as "ministers," to "every creature . . . under heaven." The Prophet Joseph Smith said that once a person is filled with this love of all mankind, he "is not content with blessing his family alone, but ranges through the whole world, anxious to bless the whole human race (*Teachings of the Prophet Joseph Smith,* 174)."

President Gordon B. Hinckley echoed this idea: "When a person is motivated by great and powerful convictions of truth, then he disciplines himself not because of demands made upon him by the Church but because of the knowledge within his heart that God lives; that he is a child of God with an eternal and limitless potential; that there is joy in service and satisfaction in laboring in a great cause" (in Conference Report, Apr. 1973, 73).

Let me share with you the story of one such young woman. Her name is LaRee, and she had the kind of faith that motivated her to share the gospel with others, not because she had to, but because she wanted to.

LaRee grew up in Lehi, Utah. Her father was an abusive alcoholic, but her mother was a good woman who did her best to raise LaRee in the Church. Across the street from LaRee lived a quiet girl named Susie.

Susie and other members of her family did not attend church, which caused her to feel left out in a predominantly LDS community. She was so small for her age that she had not been allowed to attend kindergarten, and when she turned six, she was immediately put into first grade. She fell behind because she didn't know the routine of school, the alphabet, or any of the things the other children had learned the previous year in kindergarten. To make matters worse, she had a severe stuttering disorder. All of these things made her want to sit in the back of the room and try not to be noticed.

One day a knock came at Susie's door. Because her mother was partially deaf and Susie couldn't talk without stuttering, they would purposely ignore knocks at the door. This time, however, the knocking didn't stop. Susie finally went to the door and opened it. Standing on her porch was LaRee, the girl from across the street.

"Susie, do you want to go to church with me?" LaRee asked.

Susie was caught off guard. She hated wearing dresses. And what if someone asked her a question?

"No, that's okay. Thanks, though." Susie said, and she abruptly shut the door.

Would you go back if you were LaRee?

Susie was a little surprised to find LaRee at her door the next week. *What, again?* she thought. *Didn't she get the message? What can I say to her this time?*

"Susie, it really is fun at church—I think you would like it. Don't you want to come?" LaRee asked.

"No," Susie said, quickly shutting the door.

Fortunately for Susie, LaRee didn't give up. For an entire year, in quiet determination, LaRee walked across the street *every week* and invited Susie to go to church with her. And Susie just kept saying no.

For a time, the invitations made Susie uncomfortable. But after awhile, she began to look forward to LaRee's weekly visit. What would LaRee say today? How can I tell her no this time? Finally, the day came that Susie put on a dress and waited for LaRee's knock at the door. When Susie opened the door, LaRee was surprised! "Uh—are you going somewhere, Susie?"

"Yes! I'm going to church with you," Susie said with a sparkle in her eyes.

Everyone at church was nice to Susie! The bishop shook her hand. Her teacher greeted her warmly and spoke reassuring words to her. She was made to feel entirely welcome and at home.

More than forty years have passed since that fateful day in Susie's life. She became a faithful member of the Church. Through her example and influence, other members of her immediate family also came to the Lord.

Susie eventually met a young man, and they were sealed in the Salt Lake Temple. They now have seven children, all of whom are faithful and active in the Church. Their three sons have all served full-time missions, and at the time of this writing the youngest is serving in the Dominican Republic.

Susie is my mother, and I am the oldest of those three sons. I am a member of The Church of Jesus Christ of

Latter-day Saints today because LaRee continued in her faith, "grounded and settled," and would not be "moved away from the . . . gospel, which" she had "heard." I will be grateful to her forever for not giving up on my mother. Because she persisted in love and faith, our entire family is blessed with the sweetness of the gospel.

My friends, go forward with faith! Help the Susies in your world get closer to the Savior. Don't be afraid of them. We shouldn't offend people, but we should love them enough to be patient yet persistent, extending to them the same kind of love and kindness the Lord would if he were in your place.

Like Peter, we can continue in the beginnings of our faith through trial and error until we become "grounded and settled." By the power of the Holy Ghost and the forgiveness of the Lord, we can become one of those who would not be moved from their hope in the gospel. And, like Peter, Paul, and others, we can become ministers through whom the gospel can be preached to all the world as we stand as witnesses of God in all things, times, and places. May this be our hope, may this be our faith, and may this be our love of God and of all men as we move forward in faith in Jesus Christ, our Savior.

Ronald Bartholomew was born and reared in Lehi, Utah. After serving a mission to Pusan, Korea, he met his wife, Kristen, while they were both working at the Missionary Training Center. They are the parents of six children. Brother Bartholomew attended BYU, where he received a bachelor's degree in Korean language and a master's degree in International Relations. He has served as stake Young Men president and has taught seminary for the past sixteen years. He loves walking with his wife, bicycling, woodworking, gardening, working on computers, and (especially) eating gummi bears.

2

ALWAYS REMEMBER

Scott Anderson

It was a small class, and I was one of only sixteen students. The cost of tuition had pressed my meager budget to the limit, so, to get my money's worth, I was trying to learn all I could. One day at the end of class the teacher announced, "Next time we meet, we will be playing show-and-tell, so bring something that is meaningful to you to share with the class."

What? We are going to play show-and-tell in my college class? That's a kindergarten game!

As I left campus and headed to work I thought, *Why am I wasting my time in this class?* But, then, I began to think about the possibilities. Many members of my class were not members of the Church, and I had just been home from my mission for a short while. Maybe I could share my flip chart with them and briefly review all six discussions! Then again, maybe not. But, what if I shared the 1870 edition of the old German Bible that I had been given by a family that I had baptized on my mission?

With Bible in hand, I slipped into class two days later, prepared to share a glimpse into my mission. What followed was an experience I would never forget. Students shared things such as photos, grass skirts from Hawaii (that is a story for another day!), and one student even brought a football. About forty minutes after class had begun, a fellow classmate came into the room. She listened as two of the others showed their treasures and described their significance. When they were finished, the teacher called on the young lady and asked if she had forgotten the assignment. She assured him that she had not forgotten but that she had been walking around campus for the previous forty minutes trying to decide if she had the courage to share with us what mattered most to her.

Then she reverently held up a small gold ring. I still remember the sympathy I felt for her as she fought back the tears and shared her story:

"I was three years old at the time. My mother came to tuck me into bed and stayed for a long time. She cried and told me she loved me, then said as she tied this ring around my little wrist, 'No matter what happens, always look at this ring and remember that there is a mother in the world who loves you very much!'

"When I woke up the next morning, she was gone. It was some time before my grandmother came by and helped me pack my things. Within a week, I was in an orphanage and was experiencing challenges that I had never known of before. I was lonely and afraid. I had many questions and a constant feeling that my mother would return, but I didn't know when. Morning after morning, I awoke alone—lost and confused. This went on for months, until one day I was taken from the crowded commons room and escorted into the office.

"An American couple who were in Germany serving in the military were waiting to meet me. They spoke very little German, and it was difficult to understand what was happening. However, before many hours had passed, I was riding with them in their car and had been told they were to be my new parents. I was frightened and cried and cried. As it turned out, they were the kindest, most wonderful people that any child could hope to have as parents.

"All the time I was growing up, my ring remained a

constant reminder that somewhere in the world I had another mother who loved me. I felt compelled to return someday to try to find her. That desire became a driving force in my life. During high school, I didn't participate in other activities because I was working to save the money to go to Europe to search for my other family. After many years of constant effort, as a graduation trip, I traveled to Europe. I had researched carefully and knew the town and directions to my family homestead. So, I left my tour group at the location nearest to my birthplace and traveled on a local bus for a few hours.

"I arrived at the city and after a long walk, I climbed the hill and found the home where I had lived as a little girl. There was smoke curling up from the chimney. I realized that the home was still registered to my family's name—that in this house was the link to my roots. I sat on the hillside for hours watching the home and thinking. This moment was what I had dreamt of for years. Then, without approaching the home, I turned and walked away, never knocking on the door."

She continued, "This little ring has been a constant reminder in my life, not only that I have a birthmother who loves me, but of so much more." Then with great feeling this courageous young lady said, "When I look at this ring I am grateful for all the sacrifice it represents. You see, if my mother hadn't left me to be adopted, I might never have found The Church of Jesus Christ of Latter-day Saints. I love being a Mormon more than any other thing in my life. That is what I think about when I see this ring!"

I found out in that classroom that grown-up show-and-tell is quite a different thing than it was in kindergarten. I have never forgotten the emotional presentation given by my classmate and have often thought of how her ring was a way for her to remember her mother's love for her and her gratitude for the power of the Lord in her life.

We are lucky if we have in our lives a few symbols of the

things we treasure most. I am grateful that our Heavenly Father has given us a pair of symbols to remind us of his love for us and the gift he has given us of his son, Jesus Christ. We partake of these symbols each week as we participate in the sacrament and are given the opportunity to remember.

When the Savior first blessed and administered the sacrament to his beloved disciples, I can only imagine his thoughts and feelings. He knew he was about to leave them and that they would face great challenges in his absence. How could he help them remember him in their greatest times of need? How could he ensure that his Spirit would always be with them?

As the Passover feast was coming to a close, the Savior took bread and blessed and broke it. He gave it to his disciples, saying, "Take, eat, this is my body. And he took the cup, and gave thanks, and gave it to them, saying, Drink ye all of it; For this is my blood of the new testament, which is shed for many for the remission of sins" (Matthew 26:26–28). What greater constant reminder could there be than bread, the staff of life, and water, the most common liquid on earth? These two sustain our lives and so are appropriate reminders of the Savior's role as the Bread of Life and the Living Water.

In 3 Nephi in the Book of Mormon, we are told the Savior administered the sacrament twice to help the people always remember. Can you imagine the thoughts that went through the minds of our Nephite brothers and sisters as they partook of the sacrament after he was gone? They had had the sacred privilege of thrusting their hands into his side and reverently touching the prints of the nails in his hands and feet. He had also manifested his great love for them by healing their sick and blessing their children. They had the physical evidence of his reality and resurrection and had partaken directly of his love. How can we, who were not present to feel the prints of the nails in his hands, remember him always?

Elder Dallin H. Oaks gives us a key to remembering our Savior. He states: "To remember means to keep in memory. In the scriptures, it often means to keep a person in memory, together with associated emotions like love, loyalty, or gratitude. The stronger the emotion, the more vivid and influential the memory."

Elder Oaks gives three examples:

1. "Most of us have the clearest memories of our mortal parents, who gave us birth and nurtured us through childhood. This kind of memory does not dim with the passing years, but with wisdom and perspective becomes ever more meaningful. As I grow older, I think more frequently of my father and my mother. I will always remember them."

2. "Shortly before my wife was to give birth to our first child, we learned that the baby must be born by cesarean section. I was then a student at Brigham Young University, going to school full time and working almost full time. From my meager earnings, a little over $1.00 an hour, we had saved enough money for the hospital and doctor bills, but nothing in our plans or emotions had prepared us for this shocking announcement. We scarcely knew what a cesarean birth was, and we feared the worst.

"A few days later we faced our ordeal. After what seemed an eternity, I stood at a window in the hospital hallway, looking into a basket containing our firstborn. The joy of seeing her and knowing that my beloved companion had survived the operation was inexpressible. As I experienced that moment, I became aware of a stranger standing beside me. He introduced himself as Dr. N. Frederick Hicken, the surgeon who had come from Salt Lake City to perform the operation. His presence reminded me that a surgeon's fee had not been in our plans, and I began to ask him if I could pay his fee over a period of time. 'Don't worry about that, young man,' he said in a kindly way. 'This is one from the Hickens to the Oakses.' Before I could stammer a thank-you, he was gone.

"I was filled with wonder at this unexpected gift. Our benefactor must have known my father, a young medical doctor who died when I was a boy. He must have given us this gift because of something my father had done. I marveled at the goodness of this man who had come to us in our crisis and had, without recompense, used his powers to preserve the lives of those I loved. The emotion of that moment made the memory indelible. The name of that doctor is precious to me. I will always remember him.

3. "Some time ago, someone praised me for something I had done. Even as I received that compliment I knew I did not deserve it. The credit belonged to wise and wonderful teachers who had taught me what to do and how to do it. My teachers were memorable. I shudder to think what I would have lost if teachers had not helped me want to learn and then taught me what I needed to know. I will always be grateful to my teachers. I will always remember them.

"By now you must surely realize that I have given these three examples because the reasons why I will always remember these persons are related to the reasons why we should always remember Jesus Christ: He is our Creator, our Redeemer, and our Teacher" (*Ensign,* May 1988, 30–31).

One Sunday during the presentation of the sacrament, our children (who were quite young at the time) made a little disturbance, and I realized that I hadn't shared with them sufficient understanding of why we remember the Savior in this important way. I also had a prompting of what I needed to do to help them.

The next night our wonderful neighbors agreed to spend family home evening with us. We shared a brief video presentation about the Savior's life and then headed for the cemetery in our little town. As we quietly gathered around a little graveside, a spirit of reverence settled on our group. Sweet Sister Dunn began to share her memories of her daughter Emily.

She told us that during her three-year-old birthday party, Emily became quite sick. Brother and Sister Dunn took their young daughter to the doctor and were sent home with some pain medication for her to take. However, she became even more sick during the night, and they ended up taking her this time to the hospital emergency room. It was discovered that her appendix had ruptured and that the infection was running throughout her body. Only those who have watched a loved one suffer can imagine the struggle they went through.

At about 2:00 A.M., while standing outside the intensive care unit, Sister Dunn pleaded with Heavenly Father for her little one's life. She heard a quiet question: "Do you have enough faith to ask for Emily to live?" As she searched her deepest feelings she knew that she could answer "Yes, yes I do!"

Then came the second question: "Do you have enough faith to let her go?" Hours later she was still struggling within to find the strength to honestly answer. Finally, after many hours, peace filled her heart and she was able to answer, "Yes, I do." Moments later the doctor informed her that Emily had passed away.

Bishop Dunn had been quietly standing next to his wife in the cemetery. As she finished her beautiful testimony of faith and peace, he began to share his feelings. Following Emily's passing, he had not had a peaceful experience at first. He had felt lonely and empty. He described the way Emily would greet him at the front door with some new, exciting discovery as he arrived home from work each day. Then she would wrap her little hand around his thumb and drag him out into the yard to find a new flower or a beautiful plant. He said that after she died, he didn't even want to go in the front door. It was just too hard.

Then, about a month after her death, he had a dream. In his dream he was in a crowded room. He heard Emily's voice, and she came to him, wrapped her hand around his thumb, and invited him to follow her. They made their way through the crowd and came to a door. She opened it and pulled him through it into a room. As the door closed behind them, Emily let go of her father's thumb and in a few short steps was enfolded in the loving arms of the Savior. Bishop Dunn said that he awoke on a pillow that was wet with tears, and as he shared that sacred experience with us—of seeing his Emily at peace, cradled in the Savior's arms—he testified that he also felt the Savior's love and finally found the peace that had eluded him.

It was a moving and beautiful experience that day in the cemetery. The Spirit of the Lord was present, and our children felt it. It was a perfect time to explain to them that every week we are invited to attend another sacred memorial service, one where another Father wants to share with us insights and information about the life and death of his Beloved Son. We discussed the importance of listening to what the Lord has to say to us during sacrament time. And we pointed out how much we would miss if we were to talk or not pay attention.

We all agreed that we would try very hard during the sacrament to understand what our Heavenly Father would like to teach us and to think harder about what it means to renew our sacred covenants with him.

The next week as we were singing the sacrament hymn, I whispered to the children a reminder of our experience in the cemetery. It made a difference—not only for them but for me.

Each of you has had some kind of experience in which you have felt the Spirit. Perhaps that tender feeling has come to you during EFY, seminary, family home evening,

Young Men or Young Women meetings, sacrament meeting, Sunday School, or while reading the scriptures (feasting on the word), praying, doing service, preparing for a mission and temple marriage, or attending the temple. As we recall such experiences, they give us courage and faith to do our part. What is our part? Our part is to be willing to take his name upon us, keep his commandments, and always remember him (see Moroni 4:3). As Elder Oaks said, we want to remember all that he has *created* for us, that he is our *redeemer,* and that he will be our *teacher* if we will allow him to be.

We can reap the rewards of the great show-and-tell scriptural promise: "The words of Christ will *tell* you all things what ye should do. . . . if ye will enter in by the way, and receive the Holy Ghost, it will *show* unto you all things what ye should do" (2 Nephi 32:3, 5; emphasis added). We can then know that as we do our part, the Savior will take us home with him back to our Heavenly Father.

That is my prayer for each of you.

Scott Anderson and his wife, Angell, live in Bluffdale, Utah, where they spend time working on home improvement projects, waiting for their children to come to family meetings, and ordering pizza as a reward for cleaning the house. He likes to travel, and his favorite places to go are Kentucky and Georgia to see his married children and darling grandchildren. His hobbies include teaching, writing, music, outdoor activities, sports, and building memories with his family. Brother Anderson has a Ph.D. in Marriage and Family Therapy from BYU and is currently on the faculty at the Orem Institute of Religion adjacent to Utah Valley State College. When asked to describe Scott's personality, his wife said that he is a "gratitude guru" and a "life enthusiast" who loves to serve.

3

A STONE CUT OUT WITHOUT HANDS

Randall C. Bird

It has now been almost twenty-five years since the Especially for Youth program began. I can still remember that first one. I know it's hard to believe, but there were just four of us who taught at the first EFY. I remember how close it came to being canceled. Just before the decision was reached to cancel the program, a stake sent in a registration giving us just enough participants to hold the program.That first EFY involved just under two hundred youth.

This year, 2000, there will be about forty week-long sessions held in several locations throughout the United States and Canada. We will accommodate over thirty thousand youth in those sessions. That's quite a growth in just the past twenty-five years.

Though it drives you crazy to hear an adult say, "When I was your age . . ." let's take a look at the past for just a few minutes. Not long ago while reading my e-mail messages, there was a test given that would let you determine if you were "over the hill." The test measured how well you could remember a number of things from the past. Some of the items on the test were: Blackjack chewing gum, *Howdy Doody,* soda pop machines that dispensed bottles, telephone numbers with a word prefix (such as Plaza-6933), and S&H Green stamps. Needless to say, I remembered all of them and was certified as being "over the hill."

And rightfully so. I even remember the first television that came into our neighborhood. It was such a novelty that everyone on the street would gather at the neighbor's house to watch it. The funny thing is that for many hours during the day, all that was on the screen was a "test pattern"—just a logo of the station. Yet we would sit in a room and watch it for hours on end. The miracle of *seeing* something rather than just listening to a radio was remarkable.

I remember that while serving my mission in New York City, I watched a man walk on the moon via this medium. That was such an historic event that we missionaries were allowed to witness it. I can also remember when the Missionary Training Center (MTC) was located in Salt Lake City. The building in which it was housed has long since been demolished. In those days, missionaries who had been called to foreign missions spent time learning their language in the Language Training Mission (LTM) in Provo.

So here we are living in a new millennium. Many of you attending EFY or reading this book are seniors in high school. If the Church continues to grow at a pace equal to the rate it has over the past decade, when you seniors attend your twenty-year class reunions, the Church will likely have thirty million members and eleven thousand stakes.

In 1979 Elder Neal A. Maxwell made what I believe is a prophetic statement. He said: "Now we are entering times wherein there will be for all of us as Church members, in my judgment, some special challenges which will require of us that we follow the Brethren. All the easy things that the Church has had to do have been done. From now on, it's high adventure, and followership is going to be tested in some interesting ways" ("The Old Testament: Relevancy within Antiquity," *A Symposium on the Old Testament* [Salt

Lake City: The Church of Jesus Christ of Latter-day Saints, 1979], 12).

At about the same time Especially for Youth was being founded, there were members of the Church living in sixty-six countries. The Church had twenty-three thousand missionaries, seven hundred fifty stakes, and sixteen operating temples. Temples had just been announced for Tokyo, Japan; Sao Paulo, Brazil; and Seattle, Washington. Today, with the dawning of a new millennium, there are over two thousand stakes in one hundred thirty-eight countries. President Gordon B. Hinckley recently announced additional temples will be built, bringing the total to over one hundred. Recently in Canada two temples were dedicated on the same day, marking the first time in history that's been done. The number of missionaries preaching the gospel throughout the world now numbers almost sixty thousand. Truly, it's time for high adventure.

In a recent general conference, President Hinckley described the growth of the Church. He said: "The stone was small in the beginning. It was hardly noticeable. But it has grown steadily and is rolling forth to fill the earth.

"Do you realize what we have? Do you recognize our place in the great drama of human history? This is the focal point of all that has gone before. This is the season of restitution. These are the days of restoration. This is the time when men from over the earth come to the mountain of the Lord's house to seek and learn of His ways and to walk in His paths. This is the summation of all of the centuries of time since the birth of Christ to this present and wonderful day" (*Ensign*, Nov. 1999, 74).

I don't know exactly what will happen in the next twenty years, but the scriptures are quite clear about what the future holds. We can look forward to the meeting to be held at Adam-ondi-Ahman and the battle of Armageddon (see Daniel 7:9–10; D&C 116; Revelation 16:16). We will see a time when the Dead Sea will be healed and become a living sea (see Ezekiel 47:1–12).

Many could possibly see a worldwide war followed by a thousand years of peace (see D&C 87:1–2; 101:26). We will see a temple built in Jerusalem and in Independence, Missouri (see D&C 124:36; 84:3–4). All of these events remind us that we should ready ourselves to greet the Savior upon his return to the earth he created.

One thing we all have to look forward to was described by President Lorenzo Snow. Speaking to a group of temple workers, he said: "Many of you will be living in Jackson County and there you will be assisting in building the Temple; and if you will not have seen the Lord Jesus at that time you may expect Him very soon, to see Him, to eat and drink with Him, to shake hands with Him and to invite Him to your houses as He was invited when He was here before" (in *Deseret Evening News,* 15 June 1901, 1).

I remember a movie I saw many years ago entitled *Guess Who's Coming to Dinner?* Well, can you imagine the feelings you and your family would experience if the Savior shared a meal with you? Remember the poem that asks what we would do if Jesus came to our house? Would we run around putting unacceptable magazines under the table? Dust where it has not been dusted? Pull out the Bible? Well, according to the above statement, having Jesus visit in the home may be a very real possibility for some of us in the future.

The title of my chapter, "A Stone Cut Out without Hands," comes from the book of Daniel in the Old Testament. In that book we read about King Nebuchadnezzar, the king of Babylon, who had attacked and taken prisoner the people of Jerusalem. Among the captives were Daniel and his friends. They kept their standards high and refused to drink with the king and his people.

"And in all matters of wisdom," the scripture says, "and understanding, that the king enquired of them, he found them ten times better than all the magicians and astrologers that were in all his realm" (Daniel 1:20).

King Nebuchadnezzar had a dream that he couldn't remember. It troubled him very much. He required his magicians and sorcerers to recall the dream for him and then to interpret it. Their failure to do so resulted in their deaths. Then Daniel stepped forward and assured the king that if the king would give him time, through the power of the Holy Ghost, Daniel would give him the details of his dream and the interpretation thereof. Upon receiving the revelation of the dream, Daniel said, "Blessed be the name of God for ever and ever: for wisdom and might are his; And he changeth the times and the seasons: he removeth kings, and setteth up kings: he giveth wisdom unto the wise, and knowledge to them that know understanding:

"He revealeth the deep and secret things: he knoweth what is in the darkness, and the light dwelleth with him.

"I thank thee, and praise thee, O thou God of my fathers, who hast given me wisdom and might, and hast made known unto me now what we desired of thee" (Daniel 2:20–23).

In addition to enlightening the king, Daniel let us see the future when he said, "Thou sawest till that a stone was cut out without hands, which smote the image upon his feet that were of iron and clay, and brake them to pieces" (v. 34). Then he added, "And the stone that smote the image became a great mountain, and filled the whole earth" (v. 35). Continuing the interpretation, Daniel says, "And in the days of these kings shall the God of heaven set up a kingdom, which shall never be destroyed: and the kingdom shall not be left to other people, but it shall break in pieces and consume all these kingdoms, and it shall stand for ever" (v. 44). Finally, he again points out that the stone is cut out "without hands" (v. 45).

Gerald N. Lund, an educator in the Church Educational System, mentions five things about this latter-day kingdom, which are stressed in Daniel 2: (1) The stone is cut out. (2) It is cut out "without hands"; that is, its existence is not due to any human endeavor. (3) The stone will eventually fill the earth. (4) It will break in pieces and consume all other kingdoms as it rolls forth. (5) It will stand forever ("A Stone Cut Out," *Doctrine and Covenants Symposium* [1989], 6).

Nebuchadnezzar dreamed of a great statue, made of several different materials. Daniel's interpretation of the dream follows:

As the ruling world monarch at that time, Nebuchadnezzar was recognized as the king of kings, the head of a powerful kingdom, represented by the head of gold. A succession of kingdoms would follow, each assuming in its turn, dominance in the world. History records that these were the kingdoms of Cyrus the Great, with his Medes and Persians (breast and arms of silver); replaced by the Greek or Macedonian kingdom under Philip and Alexander (belly and thighs of brass); followed by the Roman Empire (legs of iron); succeeded by a group of less dominant nations (feet and toes made of iron and clay mixed)—the kingdoms of Europe as they came into existence after the fall of the Roman Empire.

Now the real significance of the dream is in what would happen: "In the days of these kings" or kingdoms (the modern kingdoms of Europe), "the God of heaven [shall] set up a kingdom that shall never be destroyed." That kingdom, represented as a stone, would roll forth, smiting the great image and breaking it into pieces. The verse goes on to say that "the kingdom shall not be left to other people, but it shall break in pieces and consume all these kingdoms, and it shall stand for ever" (Daniel 2:44–45).

So, what is that kingdom—the kingdom of God on earth? It is The Church of Jesus Christ of Latter-day Saints, which was organized on April 6, 1830. That is the kingdom set up by God, which would never be destroyed. The Church is the stone cut out of the mountain without hands that would become a great mountain and would fill the whole earth.

Testifying that the organization of the Church was the fulfillment of Daniel's prophecy, President Spencer W. Kimball said: "History unfolded and the world powers came and went after ruling the world for a little season, but in the early nineteenth century the day had come. The new world of America had been discovered and colonized and was being settled. Independence had been gained and a constitution approved and freedom given to men, and people were now enlightened to permit truth to be established and to reign.

"No king or set of rulers could divine this history; but a young, pure, and worthy prophet could receive a revelation from God. . . .

"It came about in a regular, normal process. An inspired, fourteen-year-old boy had difficulty learning from the scriptures alone what the future was. In a dense grove of trees he sought the Lord and prayed for wisdom" (*Ensign,* May 1976, 9).

The Lord answered the boy's prayer and the Church was eventually organized. Small as it was in its infancy, consisting of only six original members, it would grow and prosper, eventually filling the whole earth. That is its prophesied destiny.

Its growth was not to be without pain. Great trials and tribulations were ahead for this little kingdom. The Saints were persecuted and driven from state to state. The Prophet Joseph was martyred at Carthage. Finally, an exodus, directed by revelation, was made to the mountains of the West where the little church was able to find refuge and gather strength. Through sacrifice, hard work, and even the shedding of the blood of the Saints, the stone is rolling forth to fill the earth.

President Gordon B. Hinckley said, "All of the history of the past had pointed to this season. The centuries with all of their suffering and all their hope had come and gone. The Almighty Judge of the nations, the Living God, determined that the times of which the prophets had spoken had arrived. Daniel had foreseen a stone which was cut out of the mountain without hands and which became a great mountain and filled the whole earth. . . .

"The stone was small in the beginning. It was hardly

noticeable. But it has grown steadily and is rolling forth to fill the earth.

"My brethren and sisters, do you realize what we have? Do you recognize our place in the great drama of human history? This is the focal point of all that has gone before. . . .

"The centuries have passed. The latter-day work of the Almighty, that of which the ancients spoke, that which the prophets and apostles prophesied, is come. It is here. For some reason unknown to us, but in the wisdom of God, we have been privileged to come to earth in a glorious age. . . .

"Given what we have and what we know, we ought to be a better people than we are. We ought to be more Christlike, more forgiving, more helpful and considerate to all around us."

Then, speaking of the new millennium that was ahead, President Hinckley added, "Let the old year go. Let the new year come. Let another century pass. Let a new one take its place. Say good-bye to a millennium. Greet the beginning of another thousand years.

"And so we shall go forward on a continuing path of growth and progress and enlargement, touching for good the lives of people everywhere for as long as the earth shall last.

"At some stage in all of this onward rolling, Jesus Christ will appear to reign in splendor upon the earth. No one knows when that will be. Not even the angels in heaven will know of the time of His return. But it will be a welcome day" (*Ensign,* Nov. 1999, 74).

The stone continues to roll forth. Each of us is part of this great work, and it's truly a time of "high adventure" as Elder Maxwell said. Nearly 60,000 missionaries proclaim the gospel truths to thousands of people in their native countries. President Spencer W. Kimball shared President Hinckley's vision, and he said of this work: "The gospel spreads to the nations of the earth in its approach toward the promise made by God through Daniel to fill the whole earth, and numerous people of all nationalities and tongues are accepting the gospel in many nations, and the Church and kingdom grow and develop, and we say to you and testify to you that it shall in Daniel's words, 'never be destroyed; and the kingdom shall not be left to other people . . . but it shall stand forever.'(Daniel 2:44.)" (*Ensign,* May 1976, 9).

I bear testimony of the truthfulness of the gospel. I know that this Church was restored through the Prophet Joseph Smith. I know it is the little stone that was cut out of a mountain without hands. I also know that it will fill the earth as was prophesied by Daniel. A statement by President Gordon B. Hinckley best summarizes my feelings: "May God bless us with a sense of our place in history and, having been given that sense, with our need to stand tall and walk with resolution in a manner becoming the Saints of the Most High, is my humble prayer in the name of Jesus Christ, amen" (*Ensign,* Nov. 1999, 74).

Randall C. Bird is the manager of seminary curriculum in the Church Educational System. A sports enthusiast, during his high school years he was named to the Idaho all-state teams in football and track, and he has served as a high school coach in both sports. Brother Bird also enjoys fishing, collecting sports memorabilia, reading, and being with his family. He and his wife, Carla, are the parents of six children and live in Layton, Utah, where Randall serves as president of the Layton Utah East Stake.

4

A MANSION OR A SHACK?

Dwight Durrant

Let's start by seeing just how smart you are. I will give you a choice, and you decide which is the best of the two choices. The choice is between two houses. Keep in mind, whichever one you choose you will have to live in for all eternity.

The first house I offer you is a beautiful mansion. You pick the style, the lot, and all the features. Make it your dream house. Don't worry about the cost or trying to keep it clean. That will all be taken care of. Now, before you make up your mind, let me offer you an alternative. I have this shed in my backyard. It was built by the construction class at Payson High School. I painted it myself. It is nice. You are welcome to live there. It will protect you from the elements. Since it is in my backyard, you are guaranteed a handsome neighbor. All right, go ahead and decide. Take your time. Choose the right.

I hope you will agree that this is a ridiculous choice. No one in their right mind would pick the shack over the mansion. It is such an easy choice. But let me use this example to make a point.

Every day of our lives we are making choices that will

determine the kind of eternal dwelling we will inhabit. The sad thing is, many of us are working our way toward the shack. Describing the hereafter, Jesus said, "In my Father's house are many mansions: . . . I go to prepare a place for you"(John 14:2). Think of it! We have a mansion waiting for us if we choose it. In fact, the way I read the scriptures, there is plenty of evidence that your name is already on the mailbox. It has been promised to you. You just have to choose it. And we choose it every day by the choices we make between right and wrong.

Let me give you some examples of what should be easy choices: Paying tithing (a mansion) or buying a new CD (a shack, if you are buying it instead of paying tithing)? Going to an R-rated movie (a shack) or one that does not contain offensive material (a mansion)? Gossipping, or building others with your words? Praying, or just climbing into bed? Going to church, or staying home to watch football? Going on a mission, or staying home? Getting married only "till death do you part," or for time and all eternity in the temple? And making a thousand other similar choices. These choices should be easy, but we often make them very difficult.

Why? Why are such easy decisions so difficult to make? May I suggest that Satan is a very skillful realtor. He can take a shack and make it seem so great. Describing the properties he offers, he uses such persuasive words as "fun," "cool," and "exciting." His advertisements read: "Drinking is cool." "This movie looks exciting." "Partying is fun." He bad-mouths his competitor by suggesting: "Church is boring." "Being goody-goody is for nerds." "Listening to your parents makes you a baby."

Satan is so good at making things that are harmful or destructive (shacks) seem fun or exciting or good. The prophet Isaiah understood this and gave us this warning: "Woe unto them that call evil good, and good evil; that put darkness for light, and light for darkness; that put bitter for sweet, and sweet for bitter!"(Isaiah 5:20). Let me illustrate with a simple story how Satan takes bitter things and makes them seem sweet.

Several years ago when my daughter Annie was about a year old, my wife had to go to a meeting and asked me to feed Annie and her older sister, Eliza. I agreed. When the time came, I sat Annie in her high chair. On my way to the cupboard where we kept the little bottles of baby food, I noticed that my wife had left a jar out on the stove. I picked it up and read the label: *Pears*. I then proceeded to feed my little girl. Normally Annie wouldn't eat very much, but she seemed to really enjoy these delicious pears. She ate most of the bottle. As a father, I felt like I had done a great job, until my wife came home. Her first question was: "Did you feed the girls?"

"Yes. Annie ate really well."

"Good. What did you feed her?"

"Those pears you left on the stove."

It was then that she gave me "The Look." Only girls know how to give this look, and my wife has it perfected. I knew I was in trouble, but I didn't know why.

"What? What did I do?"

"You fed her the pears on the stove?"

"Yes! She loved them."

"Is there any left?"

"A little. I put the bottle in the fridge."

Still giving me the look, Marci walked to the fridge. She took the bottle out and looked at it. Then she held it up and asked, "Is this what you fed her?"

"Yes, you can see. She ate almost all of it."

"Do you know what is in this bottle?"

In a smart-alecky way, I responded, "Pears."

She then said, "This is the hamburger grease left over from last night's dinner!" I suddenly felt very sick. I had fed my baby hamburger grease when I thought I was feeding her something delicious.

Sometimes Satan takes things that are absolutely disgusting, gross, and repulsive—things that will cause you great spiritual sickness—and he packages them in a way that makes them appear delicious and yummy. Disregarding the rules against deceptive advertising, he takes things such as pornography or beer or foul language and packages them in a way that makes them appear delicious. We must beware lest we eat of this hamburger grease.

Choice, or agency, is a wonderful, God-given gift, but when we make bad choices, we can't avoid the spiritual sickness that will follow. In 2 Nephi 2:27, Lehi teaches his sons about the consequences of both right and wrong choices. He says, "Wherefore, men are free according to the flesh; . . . And they are free to choose. . . ." This is where a lot of us like to stop reading. "Hey, Mom and Dad, I'm free to choose. I can do whatever I want!" But if we continue with the scripture it shows us that we are choosing between two sets of consequences: We are "free to choose liberty and eternal life . . . or to choose captivity and death [and misery]." A mansion or a shack. Satan tries to hide the fact that when we choose to commit sin we are choosing misery and captivity. I testify to you that in the long run, sin is not fun and it isn't cool. It leads to misery. As Alma taught his son Corianton, "Wickedness never was happiness" (Alma 41:10).

In 1990 the First Presidency wrote a letter to the youth of the Church, which is found in the *For the Strength of Youth* pamphlet. Our leaders said: "You cannot do wrong and feel right. It is impossible! Years of happiness can be lost in the foolish gratification of a momentary desire for pleasure. Satan would have you believe that happiness comes only as you surrender to his enticement to self-indulgence. We need only to look at the shattered lives of those who violate God's laws to know why Satan is called the 'father of all lies' (2 Nephi 2:18)."

In other words, Satan is trying to sell you a shack full of misery. Don't fall for it.

I know this sometimes seems hard, but it is worth it when you consider the rewards. Satan would have you think that it is impossible to make it to the celestial kingdom. Why even try? I asked the students in some of my seminary classes what kingdom they thought they would go to if they were to die. Most felt the terrestrial, or middle kingdom. Very few felt that they would go to the celestial kingdom. I must argue with this way of thinking. You don't have to be perfect. I believe that most of the wonderful youth of the Church are on the right path. Let me ask, what kingdom do you get baptized to enter? The celestial. Which is the only kingdom which requires temple marriage? The celestial. God isn't just playing games with us. Making it to the celestial kingdom is not some impossible hope but a very real probability. Why do you think Christ suffered in Gethsemane? So we could go to some lower kingdom? No! We don't sing songs such as "Families Can Be Together Forever" just for the fun of it. We sing it because it is a real possibility for each of us. We can make it.

President Ezra Taft Benson said: "I think that our Heavenly Father expects the youth of our Church to become exalted in the celestial kingdom. . . . We are not striving for the lower kingdoms. We are not candidates for the telestial or terrestrial kingdoms. The young people of this Church are candidates for the celestial kingdom" (*The Teachings of Ezra Taft Benson* [1988], 560).

On another occasion, President Benson said, "I would like to express the hope which [I] have for you, which is so real, that you will be exalted in the highest degree of glory in the celestial kingdom" (*The Teachings of Ezra Taft Benson,* 535). We can make it. Through our baptism, temple marriage, the priesthood, the help of the Holy Ghost, and especially through repentance and the

Atonement of Christ, the way has been opened. We can and will make it. But, each of us must choose it.

The everyday choices we make are so important because they ultimately lead to even bigger, more important choices. Allow me to share with you the two biggest choices of my life: the choice I made to go on a mission and the girl I chose to marry. First, my mission.

As a young boy I would often accompany my father as he went on many speaking assignments. One of his favorite themes was missionary work. Each time he spoke on this subject he would always include a promise to the young men. He often stated: "Missions make a man more handsome." Then he would follow that up with what he felt was undeniable evidence, "And I've been on three missions." I heard him say that many, many times and though I saw what my dad's three missions had done for his looks, I still felt that there may be some truth to this theory.

While I was in high school, I would often stare into the mirror and say to myself, "I've got to go on a mission." Finally, the time came, and I was called to serve in the Ohio Columbus Mission. I tried to serve diligently in order that I might be blessed with the good looks that my father had promised. I would often look in the mirror and wonder if my mission was working. It was hard to tell on a day-to-day basis. Soon my mission was coming to an end. My father was coming to Ohio to pick me up. Who better to judge if my mission had worked than the man who had taught me this principle?

As he stepped off the plane, I greeted him with a big warm hug. Then, anxiously, I stepped back a few paces and asked, "Well, Dad, did it work? Did my mission make me more handsome?" He looked me over for a moment, then replied, "Well, Son, I guess it doesn't work in all cases." I was devastated. But you can tell from the picture included with this chapter that my dad was only kidding, right?

I must admit that I don't know if my mission made me

more handsome or not, but one thing that I do know is that my mission made me much more spiritually handsome. The experiences I had in the mission field caused my spirit to mature in ways that no other experience could have provided. I grew up spiritually. I loved my mission. To decide to go was a great choice. Great blessings come to those who serve missions. Young men, you must go. The Lord has commanded it through prophets.

President Spencer W. Kimball said: "So let us make [a] rule—that every boy *ought* to go on a mission. There may be some who can't, but they *ought* to go on a mission. . . . This is your privilege. This is your duty. This is a command from the presidency of the Church and from your Lord" (*The Teachings of Spencer W. Kimball* [1982], 551–52).

I can think of only two reasons why a healthy, worthy young man wouldn't go: he either doesn't believe in God or doesn't love God. Going on a mission and faithfully performing your labors will put you on the path toward one day inheriting a mansion in the celestial kingdom. Who knows, maybe it will even make you more handsome.

The next great choice I made occurred after my arrival home from my mission. I had a goal to be married within a year, and I began a diligent search for a wife. I dated as often as I could convince a girl to go out with me. To prove to you how hard I was trying, I even went to BYU, often referred to as the "happy hunting grounds." A year passed, and I had not yet met my goal. I hadn't even had a girlfriend. I was not discouraged; the second year would be my year. It soon passed and still not even a girlfriend. The pressure grew ever greater, and I began to get nervous. I had only one more year at BYU. It was at the beginning of my third year that tragedy struck my life. My *younger* brother got married. Now, I am a very competitive person, and to have my little brother beat me at *anything* is bad news. I can't describe how it felt to go to my younger brother's wedding reception and have every person I knew say something like,

"Well, little brother beat you to it," or "When is it your turn?" I was determined to search even harder than ever.

It was about this time that I met Marci. We were in the same ward at BYU. One Sunday, after I had participated in passing the sacrament, I noticed an empty seat next to her. I had seen her around but I didn't know her name. I asked permission to take the seat, and while the talks were being introduced, I decided to use a line on her right there in sacrament meeting. Now I know some of you are thinking that it's not appropriate to use pick-up lines in church, but I would like to remind you that one of the highest ordinances of the gospel is temple marriage.

So I turned to her and said, "Don't you owe me dinner?" What a dumb line. She didn't even know my name. Of course she didn't owe me dinner, but she felt so sorry for me that she agreed. I said, "How about right after sacrament meeting?" She said okay.

When we got to her apartment, to her embarrassment, we were not able to find any food in her cupboards. I felt bad, so I said, "My parents live just a couple of blocks from here. They always have food at their house and they are at church right now. If we hurry, we can go get some of their food before they get home." We raided my parents' kitchen, then went back to Marci's apartment to fix dinner there. After dinner, we spent the rest of the day together. Finally, at about 9:30 P.M., I decided I had better go. But before leaving, I asked Marci for a date. She accepted, and we had so much fun on the first date that I asked her out again and then again. It was like a new world record for me. I started to think that maybe I had found the right one.

However, there was a problem: Marci already had a boyfriend. Nevertheless, I decided that she was worth going after. When I asked her out, she would always say yes, and we would have a great time together. But it seemed that wherever I went, I would see her with this other guy. I had grown to like her a lot, and seeing her with another guy was very frustrating to me. I couldn't stand the thought of her having another boyfriend. I think this is called "two-timing."

Finally, I decided I couldn't take the pain any longer. I told her she had to make up her mind—that it was going to be either him or me. She promised that she would decide soon. It was shortly after giving her this ultimatum that we were sitting together waiting for sacrament meeting to begin. I asked her if she had made up her mind, and she responded that she had not. It was then that a miracle happened. The organist began playing the introduction to the opening hymn. This hymn has since become my favorite. Of all the hymns that could have been chosen that day, the one that we began to sing was "Choose the Right." Hey, I'm no dummy. I picked up on it right away and began to sing extra loud. I needed to send her a message because, obviously, I was the right choice.

I kept glancing at her, but it wasn't really working. She didn't appear to be feeling the inspiration. As the second verse was being sung, I was inspired to change the words just a little. Instead of singing "choose the right," my first name being Dwight, I began to sing at the top of my voice: "Choose D'wight, choose D'wight." I guess it worked because she soon told the other guy she had made "D'wight" choice. Marci and I have been together ever since.

Now let me tell you why choosing Marci was such a great choice for me. First, it was the right time, or D'wight time. Even though it took me a long time, I hadn't rushed into anything; I was old enough and mature enough to be ready for such a big commitment. Second, she was the right girl: Marci had very high standards and a strong testimony of the gospel. She also had a strong desire to be a mother. Third, we were married in the right place, the Salt Lake Temple, a house of God. Fourth, we were married by the right authority, the sacred sealing power of the priesthood. This assures us that if we are faithful to our covenants, we will be married for all eternity and receive a mansion in the celestial kingdom. We don't have to settle for anything less (a shack).

Now let me tell you about one of the worst choices I ever made in my life. This wasn't a sin. It was just a bad choice. However, I would like you to relate it to sin. During my sophomore year in college, I was reading in the BYU newspaper and came across an ad that captured my attention. It read: "Winter special, parachuting, one-half off." Now I'm not the type that would ever do anything as crazy as jump out of an airplane. Only one thing could make me do it—peer pressure. Peer pressure is a powerful force that makes shacks seem fun and exciting.

I showed the ad to my roommate Crazy Robb. I knew he could pressure me into it. When I handed him the ad, he said just two words: "I'm there." I found myself echoing his words: "*I'm* there."

That next Saturday, five of the six people who lived in our apartment headed out to take parachuting lessons. Our lessons began at 8:00 A.M. on a cold winter's day. During that day our instructors taught us many things about parachuting. The closer we got to jumping, the more nervous I became. Finally, it was time, and they asked who wanted to go first. Robb went crazy. He yelled: "I'm first! I'm first!" Then he announced, "Durrant's second." I didn't really want to go, but I didn't say a thing as they put the chutes on our backs and loaded Robb and me and one other friend into the first plane. I have to tell you, I was scared to death. As we circled higher and higher, my fear grew greater and greater. I sat in my corner of the plane with my eyes closed (because you're supposed to have your eyes closed when you are praying). I was repenting of everything I had ever done because I was convinced I was about to die. About this time, the jump master kicked the door of the plane open with his foot. The sound startled me, and the wind began rushing through the plane. It was the single scariest moment of my life.

Robb went first. When I saw his chute open, great joy filled my soul, but fear soon replaced it as the jump master instructed me to slide over to the door. He then shouted, "Get out." Reluctantly, I grabbed hold of a little bar under the wing and got out of the plane. Hanging on to this little bar, I was now flying like Superman. Actually, it was more like I was flapping violently in the wind. I turned toward the jump master and heard the word "Go!" My grip remained tight. I couldn't let go. I was hanging on for dear life. After a moment, he yelled very loudly, "Go!" He scared me so badly that I let go.

At this point, I forgot everything I had been taught. I was supposed to arch my body backward, but I had no idea what position my body was in. The jump master later told me that I curled up into a ball. I was supposed to count to five as I fell. If I could have counted to one, I would have done it, but at that desperate moment in my life, I had no concept of counting. Fortunately, the plane pulls your rip cord for you, and I felt a tug on my shoulders. I was then supposed to look up and say out loud, "I am checking my canopy." Instead of doing so, I was just trying to breathe. From the time the jump master had said, "Get out," I don't think I had taken a breath.

The first thing I finally remembered to do was to check for the wind sock at the airport to see which way the wind was blowing in order that I might land in the proper direction. Landing against the wind slows you down to help ensure a soft landing. The instructors had told us that at that point in our descent we might go ahead and have a little fun by pulling on the tabs above our heads, which would make us turn. I pretended like I was having fun, but I want you to know that I was having zero amount of fun.

Before I knew it, the ground was getting very near. This would not have been a big problem except that I was facing the direction the wind was blowing. This would cause me to land hard and fast—not a good thing. I remembered the instructor saying that you should never be turning when you land, so I had to make a decision: should I come in for a fast landing or should I risk landing in the middle of a turn? I opted for the fast landing.

As I came in, I felt that I had perfect form: feet close together, knees tightly together, and head tucked safely into my shoulders. However, after it was all over, my friends (if I can call them that) asked, "Why were you kicking your legs during your landing?" They said that my legs were flying wildly as I came in. So there I was, getting closer and closer to the earth, coming in for a landing—facing the wrong direction, going much too fast, and exhibiting terrible form.

Our instructors had also taught us not to look at the ground as we came in for our landing because it would deceive us. Not me, I wanted to see when I was going to hit. I stared at the ground as it got closer and closer until finally my feet touched down. At this point I was supposed to tuck and roll sideways. However, I learned something about the laws of physics that day. Because I was going so fast, I fell straight forward. My face finally stopped my momentum by slamming into the frozen ground. Painfully, I picked myself up, gathered up my chute, and headed back toward the airport. I wanted to rub my throbbing face, but with my whole class watching, I didn't do so. The greatest pain came as I heard them laughing at me as I walked toward them.

I had done everything wrong. I had not followed the instructions I had been given and as a result, I had fallen flat on my face. This is what happens when we make wrong decisions in life. I call them "spiritual face-plants." When we make bad choices, go against the teachings of our parents and leaders, or allow our peers to influence us negatively, we spiritually fall flat on our faces. It hurts. Sin hurts. It is not fun. It is not cool. We need to pick ourselves up, brush ourselves off (repent), and never do it again.

"Choose the right when a choice is placed before you." Don't fall for Satan's deceptions (shacks). Your Heavenly Father loves you. That is why he allows you to choose. That is why he sent his Son to help you overcome the spiritual face-plants in your life. He will never serve you hamburger grease. The gospel is delicious and wonderful. It makes you more handsome and beautiful.

As we choose to live the gospel, we can be sure of one day receiving the mansion that has been prepared for us. We can do it!

Dwight Durrant teaches seminary at Payson High School. He and his wife, Marci, have four children: Eliza, Annie, Cami, and Will. He currently serves in a bishopric of a BYU singles ward. He has run four marathons and has a goal to run 2,000 kilometers (1,240 miles) in the year 2000 (2KnY2K). He served in the Ohio Columbus Mission and graduated from BYU and received his master's degree from Utah State.

5

BORN AGAIN

Sue Egan

Verily, verily, I say unto thee, Except a man be born again, he cannot see the kingdom of God (John 3:3).

When Michael was six years old, he announced to his family that he had taken his final bath. According to Michael, baths were a huge waste of both his time and energy. So he was finished. Done. Cleansed for life. No amount of reasoning could change his mind. Phrases such as "bacteria laden" and "odor ridden" failed to persuade him otherwise.

Mike's mother had a choice to make. Three different approaches crossed her mind. One, she could force him to bathe by physically tossing him into the tub each evening. Two, she could escalate the battle by taking away treasured privileges. Or, three, resort to that time-tested method that desperate parents sometimes resort to—bribery. For better or worse, she chose method number three. She promised Michael that each time he peacefully agreed to bathe, she would let him dye the bathwater the color of his choice. Believe it or not, it worked. In fact, Michael now looked forward to bath time. Each evening Mike would choose a color. His mom would put a few drops of food coloring in the water and presto! Bath time was now both functional and entertaining.

Unfortunately, all this was done without the knowledge or consent of Michael's father. One night Mike's mom had a meeting at the ward that kept her away during his bath time. Unaware of the new colored water policy, Michael's father, Jeff, began running a bath for Mike. Michael came into the bathroom, began peeling off his socks, and enthusiastically shouted, "Dad, tonight I choose green!" Jeff looked at his son with a blank stare, so Michael clarified, "Dad, tonight I choose the color green for my bath."

Aside from the sound of running water, there was dead silence in the room. Finally, in exasperation Mike asked, "Dad, don't you know where to look in the kitchen for my bath-time food coloring?" Jeff was shocked.

"Son, what are you talking about? Why would we put food coloring in your bath?" So Michael told his dad the whole story. The colored bathwater bribery scandal was now out in the open. Oops.

Jeff decided that he would put an end to this silliness there and then. No colored bath tonight, no colored bath tomorrow, no colored bath ever again. Get in the water, get clean, get out. That was the new plan. Period. End of sentence. Case closed.

Succumbing to his father's approach, Mike reluctantly climbed into his boring, clear water bath. Even the few toys his dad tossed into the tub didn't placate him. This was terrible. How could he be expected to sit in this uninteresting, wet porcelain prison? Then he had an idea. He knew where his mom kept the food coloring. All he had to do was sneak out of the bathroom, make a quick getaway into the kitchen, tiptoe back into the bathroom, and dye the water himself. It was a perfect plan. Yahoo! Life was about to get good again.

Leaving a trail of water, Michael made his way to the

kitchen. Scooting a chair over to the cupboard he climbed up to where the food coloring containers were kept on the top shelf. They were hard to miss. At the rate Michael was going through food coloring, his mom had decided that the little two-inch vials that you buy at a regular supermarket weren't lasting long enough. So she went to one of those grocery warehouses where you can buy massive containers of the stuff. (Just one of those bottles will last you through the millennium.) As he stood on the kitchen counter, Michael was face-to-face with a quart of green dye. Bath time was about to become fun again.

Sneaking back into the bathroom, Michael took the lid off the container and spilled a few drops of the dye into the tub. The water turned a very, very pale green. He decided that a few more drops were necessary. Once again, the desired hue of green wasn't attained. *Okay, that's enough,* he thought. *I'm cold, I'm wet, and this is taking forever."* So he unscrewed the cap and poured the entire contents into the bath water. Glug-glug-glug-glug-glug-glug-glu-glu-gl-gl-ahhhh! The container was empty. And to his delight, his bath was now a brilliant shade of emerald green!

Wow! It was beautiful! As he jumped into the water he was ecstatic. The toys his dad had thrown in earlier were hidden in the depths of this wonderful opaque stuff. This was so much better than the pale shades his mother had created. Someday he would have to show his mom how much food coloring to add to make the water really exquisite.

Looking over at the bathroom counter he saw a toy that had been left next to the sink. It was Sanford, his favorite plastic shark. Surely Sanford deserved to frolic in this wonderful wet murk, so Michael climbed out of the tub for just a moment to grab the toy. As he was about to get back into the bath, he happened to glance down at his feet.

Horrors! Oh, no! Disaster! Michael discovered that he had dyed himself dark green from the waist down.

Stricken with fear, Michael cried out, "Dad, help me!" And within seconds his father stood in the doorway surveying the damage. His father's response was classic. He simply said, "Michael, it looks like you need my help to get cleaned up." And that's just what Jeff did. I don't know how he did it, but when I saw Michael a few weeks later at the neighborhood swimming pool, no traces of green remained.

Each of us is like Michael in a way. We are all stained with sin, and we need our Heavenly Father's help to get it off. He has provided the way for us to become clean again. Through the Atonement of his Son, Jesus Christ, each of us can become "holy, without spot" (Moroni 10:33). There is no other way. We can't get clean by ourselves. "No flesh . . . can dwell in the presence of God, *save it be through the merits, and mercy, and grace of the Holy Messiah* (2 Nephi 2:8; emphasis added). This cleansing transformation that can take place in our lives is described in the scriptures as being "born again." Some other phrases used to describe this spiritual rebirth are: "changed from [a] carnal and fallen state, to a state of righteousness" (Mosiah 27:25), "the baptism of fire" (2 Nephi 31:13), "converted" (Luke 22:32; see Bible Dictionary, s. v. Conversion, 650), and experiencing "a mighty change" (Alma 5:12). This "mighty change" occurs when we actually receive the Holy Ghost and are cleansed from sin.

Nephi teaches us about the pattern we must follow in our lives to have this sanctifying process take place. He encourages us to "follow the Son, with full purpose of heart, acting no hypocrisy and no deception before God, but with real intent, repenting of your sins, witnessing unto the Father that ye are willing to take upon you the name of Christ, by baptism . . . then shall ye receive the

Holy Ghost; yea, then cometh the baptism of fire and of the Holy Ghost" (2 Nephi 31:13).

In other words, we must have faith in Christ, repent of our sins, receive the ordinances of baptism and confirmation, and then live worthily so that we can *receive* the Holy Ghost. This is a path we must follow throughout our entire lives, enduring to the end. Nephi reminds us, "Unless a man shall endure to the end, in following the example of the Son of the living God, he cannot be saved" (2 Nephi 31:16).

Nephi teaches further, "Wherefore, ye must press forward with a steadfastness in Christ, having a perfect brightness of hope, *and a love of God and of all men"* (2 Nephi 31:20; emphasis added). As we press forward and experience this sanctifying process in our lives, we change. We are filled with love for both our Heavenly Father and our fellow man. Among other things, this love motivates us to do whatever it takes to serve the Lord and have his Spirit with us.

When we begin to think in these terms, the words of the sacramental covenant, "that [we] are willing to take upon [us] the name of thy Son, and always remember him and keep his commandments which he has given [us]," become more than just familiar words we are accustomed to hearing each week. They invite us to adopt a way of life—always remembering the Savior with a heart full of gratitude, motivated by love to keep his commandments so that the glorious promise "that [we] may always have his Spirit to be with [us] . . ." can be fulfilled (D&C 20:77).

My eleven-year-old daughter, Ali, loves her big sister, Jen, with all her heart. Last summer Jen and her husband, Dan, moved to Spokane, Washington, so that Dan could attend law school. Ever since their move, Ali has yearned for a reunion with her sister. So, Ali decided that she was going to save money for the plane fare to Washington by doing odd jobs for members of our family. She helped me restore order to my files, cleaned out the storage room, and straightened her dad's office. Ali even took on the *enormous* task of cleaning her older brother Josh's bedroom. (That was a job that would bring even the most accomplished homemaker to her knees!) Her willingness to be the family maid had netted her $30. But she needed $170. The money wasn't adding up quickly enough, so Ali resorted to advertising her enterprise. Each member of the family was handed a note written in impeccable fifth grade penmanship. It read as follows:

> *Ali's Cleaning Service*
> *Hours:*
> *Monday through Thursday 3:30–6:30*
> *Friday and Saturday 10:00–6:30*
> *(Remember, I do not have school on Friday this week!) Ali is already booked on the following days: Monday–Mom, Tuesday–Josh, Wednesday–Dad*
>
> *Please sign up at her office located in her bedroom. If you already have a day booked with her, feel free to add another. First come, first served. NOTICE–She will do ANY kind of job you want her to do. Thanks for your cooperation.*

Ali loves her sister and has declared her willingness to do *anything* to be with her once again. As each of us grows in our conversion to the Savior and his gospel, we, too, will be willing to *do anything* to feel his Spirit and be worthy to return to his presence. As the father of King Lamoni was taught the gospel, he had an overwhelming desire to have the Spirit of the Lord with him, to be born of God, and to inherit eternal life (see Alma 22:15). Indeed, his longing to receive these gifts was so great that he cried out in prayer, "I will give away all my sins to know thee" (Alma 22:18).

What sins are you willing to give away to know him? Every youth in the Church should have in his or her possession a copy of the pamphlet *For the Strength of Youth.* The standards of behavior summarized in that publication are the Lord's guidelines to help you measure your conduct and devotion. For instance, the section entitled "Music and Dancing" reads: "Music can help you draw closer to your Heavenly Father. It can be used to educate, edify, inspire, and unite. However, music can be used for wicked purposes. Music can, by its tempo, beat, intensity, and lyrics, dull your spiritual sensitivity. You cannot afford to fill your minds with unworthy music. You must consider your listening habits thoughtfully and prayerfully. You should be willing to control your listening habits and shun music that is harmful" (pp. 13–14).

Have you prayed about your choice of music? Do some of your choices offend the Spirit? Are you willing to quit listening to inappropriate songs and replace them with music that is inspiring and edifying? Does your behavior measure up to the Lord's standard in music and other areas such as language, media, dating, and sexual purity?

Find your copy of *For the Strength of Youth.* (Hint! Keep a copy of the pamphlet tucked into your scriptures so it is always accessible.) Read it from cover to cover. Invite the Holy Ghost to be with you as you study each page. While reading, compare your behavior and thoughts with Heavenly Father's standard. Perhaps a feeling of peace and joy will settle over you as you recognize those parts of your behavior that are in line with the Lord's standard. Good for you! Doesn't the Spirit feel great? You are experiencing the "fruit of the Spirit" of which the apostle Paul spoke when he taught, "But the fruit of the Spirit is love, joy, peace, longsuffering, gentleness, goodness, faith" (Galatians 5:22).

Maybe there are other passages that make you feel uncomfortable, rebellious, or guilty. Chances are, those are the standards that you are not keeping. Are you like Esau, who was willing to sell his birthright for a mess of pottage? (see Genesis 25:29–34). Or are you willing to soften your heart and volunteer the sins you are willing to give away to know the Lord? Specifically, what CDs do you need to discard? What immodest articles of clothing will you remove from your wardrobe? What words will you drop from your vocabulary? What relationships will you modify or abandon so that you are in compliance with the Lord's standards? Sister Sheri Dew, second counselor in the General Relief Society Presidency, asks, "What are we willing to do, what weaknesses and indulgences will we give up to have as our personal protector and guide the constant companionship of the Holy Ghost? . . . May each one of us resolve that nothing will stand between us and the Spirit of the Lord" (*Ensign,* Nov. 1998, 96).

Even after we resolve to do whatever it takes to have his Spirit with us, we will fall short of perfection. The prophet Nephi lamented, "O wretched man that I am! Yea, my heart sorroweth because of my flesh; my soul grieveth because of mine iniquities. I am encompassed about, because of the temptations and the sins which do so easily beset me . . . nevertheless, I know in whom I have trusted. . . . My God hath been my support" (2 Nephi 4:17–20). Elder Ronald E. Poelman reminds us, "Being mortal, and despite our resolve and efforts, we will continue to fall short of perfection. However, with Nephi of old, conscious of our weaknesses, temptations, and past mistakes, we may say, 'nevertheless, I know in whom I have trusted.' (2 Ne. 4:19.) There follows a natural resolve to renew our efforts" (*Ensign,* Nov. 1993, 85).

One way we can resolve to renew our efforts is to correct our mistakes as soon as we make them. For instance, Josh is a thirteen-year-old boy in my ward. Each Sunday as the deacons take their places on the front row in the chapel, Josh is almost always the most reverent. He listens intently to who is conducting the meeting. As the sacrament song is sung, he sings purposefully. As he sings, his face reflects his love for the Lord and the gospel.

One day I remarked to Josh's mother how devoted he appears to be. She confirmed my observation. She told me that Josh has a solid testimony and a strong desire to choose the right. Yet, even though Josh loves the Lord, he isn't perfect. Like every other thirteen-year-old boy, he has moments of conflict with his mother and father. His mom confided in me that after Josh has a disagreement with his parents he usually disappears into his bedroom for a while. But inevitably, within ten or fifteen minutes, he will soften his heart, apologize, and peace is quickly restored.

As Josh is growing in the conversion process, sin makes him uncomfortable, so when he makes a mistake he moves to quickly correct it. He has learned to enjoy the sweet feeling the Holy Ghost brings, and his actions reflect his desire to maintain those feelings. Josh is not unlike the Saints in King Benjamin's day, who in response to the king's sermon about the need for spiritual rebirth cried: "We believe all the words which thou hast spoken unto us; and also, we know of their surety and truth, because of the Spirit of the Lord Omnipotent, which has wrought a mighty change in us, or in our hearts, *that we have no more disposition to do evil, but to do good continually*" (Mosiah 5:2; emphasis added).

The spiritual rebirth process is truly a miracle. Christ does for us what we could never do for ourselves. Through his Atonement and the sanctifying power of the Holy Ghost, we can be cleansed from sin and turned into a "new creature"(2 Corinthians 5:17). Through his grace we can be "spiritually begotten" of him and "become his sons and his daughters"(Mosiah 5:7). All he asks is that we go forward in faith and partake of his holy ordinances, obey his commandments, and love him with all our hearts.

The doctrine of spiritual rebirth is a glorious part of the plan of salvation offered to all who will come unto Christ. "Behold, he sendeth an invitation unto all men, for the arms of mercy are extended towards them, . . . Come unto me and ye shall partake of the fruit of the tree of life" (Alma 5:33–34).

In his concluding testimony, as he prepared to bury the gold plates, Moroni summed up the gospel of Jesus Christ by saying:

"Yea, come unto Christ, and be perfected in him, and deny yourselves of all ungodliness; and if ye shall deny yourselves of all ungodliness, and love God with all your might, mind and strength, then is his grace sufficient for you, that by his grace ye may be perfect in Christ; and if by the grace of God ye are perfect in Christ, ye can in nowise deny the power of God.

"And again, if ye by the grace of God are perfect in Christ, and deny not his power, then are ye sanctified in Christ by the grace of God, through the shedding of the blood of Christ, which is in the covenant of the Father unto the remission of your sins, that ye become holy, without spot" (Moroni 10:32–33).

Sue Egan is a homemaker and the mother of six children. She has worked for BYU Youth and Family Programs for ten years. Sister Egan is an avid student of the scriptures and is currently teaching the Gospel Doctrine Sunday School class in her ward. She and her husband, Rick, reside with their family in Salt Lake City, Utah.

6

MORE SACRED THAN LIFE ITSELF

Curtis Galke

I remember sitting in the living room at my bishop's home. I was turning twelve and having my first interview. I was excited. For years I had watched as others had blessed and passed the sacrament, now I was soon to receive the Aaronic Priesthood, and it would be my turn.

I hadn't really anticipated the direction the interview would take. We talked casually at first as the bishop asked me about family, school, and friends, but then the interview became more pointed. The bishop began asking questions about my personal purity, and I became increasingly uneasy. He used words and phrases that were unfamiliar to me, and even though I knew I was worthy to hold the priesthood, I hated the anxious feeling I was having inside. I wondered why he had to ask questions that made me feel so uncomfortable.

Though the bishops changed, I was asked pretty much the same questions during my annual worthiness interviews. Although those interviews never became entirely comfortable, I began to anticipate the kinds of things that would be asked. Over time, I began to understand why the bishop would ask questions that made me uncomfortable—he was trying to remind me of the responsibility that was mine as a priesthood holder to live within the moral boundaries the Lord has set.

Speaking about moral purity or chastity is always a challenge for leaders. It is a topic that can make both the innocent and those who have made mistakes feel uneasy. If not carefully and sensitively approached, the subject can quickly be reduced to a level that wouldn't be consistent with its sacred nature. Some young people have complained that they hear too often about the law of chastity from their stake presidents, bishops, and advisers, in classes, quorums, and firesides. Working in a busy hospital emergency room, I see the consequences of immorality during every single shift that I work. I am convinced that the lessons and warnings given to the youth need to be even louder and clearer. The world in which you are growing up accepts and even promotes a destructive standard of morality that is completely different from the standard of the Lord.

To ensure that you are not confused or deceived, I want to share with you the teachings of the prophets and the scriptures on this sacred topic. The discussion will be frank and clear, in the hope that these things will give you an added weapon in your arsenal as you fight against those who would destroy your happiness, your future, even your own soul.

One of the most important lessons I have learned as a parent is that my children are more likely to obey me when I ask them to do something if I am able to give them a reason for doing what I have asked of them. "Because I'm the dad, and I say so," just doesn't seem to cut it!

My four-year-old son, Brayden, learned a hard lesson a year ago. We have a family rule that we don't jump on and off the beds or furniture in the house. I suppose that Brayden didn't think that the rule was important, or simply didn't know why we had set the rule. While some friends were visiting one evening, Brayden got wound up and jumped several times from the couch. I next heard him screaming and holding his leg.

Being the concerned dad and doctor, I examined him, used his experience to remind him to obey the family rules, and sent him off to bed. As he hobbled off to his room, my wife suggested I take him to the ER for Xrays. I thought I knew how to recognize a broken bone, but I've learned from experience that my wife is usually right, so off we went. Brayden *had* broken his leg and was in a cast for the next six weeks, which included all of the Christmas holidays. Too small to use crutches, he would scoot himself around the house on his rear end. He learned the hard way why we have silly family rules, but even more importantly he learned that disobeying rules often results in painful consequences.

Why then does the Lord and his Church set such a strict standard for morality? Why is it important to obey the law of chastity? We know that the spirit and body together make up the soul of man (see D&C 88:15) and that if the spirit and body are separated, man cannot receive a fulness of joy (see D&C 93:34). Our bodies then are key to the plan of salvation and eternal progression of our soul. Without a body we will never obtain the happiness that our Father has intended for us. Writing on this topic, Elder Jeffrey R. Holland emphasizes the sacredness of the body: "One who toys with the God-given . . . body of another toys with the very soul of that individual, toys with the central purpose and product of life, 'the very key' to life . . . In trivializing the soul of another (please include the word *body* there) we trivialize the atonement which saved that soul and guaranteed its continued existence. And when one toys with the Son of Righteousness . . . one toys with white heat and a flame hotter and holier than the noonday sun. You cannot do so and not be burned" (*On Earth As It Is in Heaven* [1989], 185).

When you understand the law of chastity in that light, it is little wonder that the scriptures teach: "These things [sexual transgressions] are an abomination in the sight of the Lord; yea, most abominable above all sins save it be the shedding of innocent blood or denying the Holy Ghost" (Alma 39:5). As early as the onset of this dispensation, long before the world's moral standards would sink as low as they have, the Prophet Joseph Smith taught that immorality would be the plaguing sin of this generation (see *Journal of Discourses,* 8:55).

That leaves those of us who understand the gospel without excuse, but consider those who are left to sort out right from wrong without the benefit of any understanding of divine law or modern revelation. No wonder they are confused and lost. Tune into prime-time television and you will see the top-rated shows normalize sexual activity in casual dating and legitimize living together without the wholehearted commitment of marriage. Moreover, the scripts and storylines make it appear that if you believe otherwise, you are hopelessly out of touch, old-fashioned, and uptight. Everywhere we turn, we are bombarded by advertisements, movies, and music lyrics that reflect the same worldly standard. Make no mistake about it, the world in which you are living is much different than the one in which your parents grew up.

Some who profess to study human behavior would have us believe that the current disregard for decency and purity is nothing more than a social evolution into a newer standard. Surveying these trends and attitudes, President Ezra Taft Benson condemned the erosion of previous values, teaching that this "so-called new morality . . . is nothing more than immorality" (*The Teachings of Ezra Taft Benson* [1988], 279). President Spencer W. Kimball taught: "The world may countenance premarital sex experiences, but the Lord and his church condemn in no uncertain terms *any* and *every* sex relationship outside of marriage" (*The Teachings of Spencer W. Kimball* [1982], 265; emphasis added). These plain statements provide a clear, understandable standard, which allows absolutely no room for any rationalization, compromise, or justification. Members of the Church who attempt to compile lists of what we can and cannot do and remain morally clean are wasting their time and walking on shaky ground. Is there any way to misunderstand President Kimball's declaration? *Any* and *every* are completely inclusive.

DECIDE NOW TO REMAIN CHASTE

With that in mind, I want to share with you four ideas of how to prepare to prevent a tragedy. First, decide *now* to be chaste. You need to make a firm commitment to live the Lord's law of chastity in the cold light of day—before you get into a compromising or tempting situation. The emotions we are talking about are such that once unleashed they are difficult to tame or control. Decide *now*—before your judgment is clouded and your resistance is down—to be virtuous and to keep yourself clean.

Not long ago I had a fifteen-year-old girl come to see me in the emergency room. She told me that she was pregnant for the second time and had come to the ER seeking treatment for an infectious, sexually transmitted disease, which she had contracted from her boyfriend. She spoke of drugs and alcohol, parties and friends. As we talked, I noticed that there was no warmth in her voice and no light in her eyes.

In her mind she was an independent young woman, doing what she wanted to do. After all, it was "her body," and she was old enough to make her own decisions. If she had understood the gospel, she might have insisted she was only exercising her agency, and that would have been true. We are all at liberty to choose how we will behave and what we will do. But that doesn't mean that we are free from the consequences of our behavior. One of the basic teachings of the gospel is "whatsoever a man soweth, that shall he also reap" (Galatians 6:7). This young woman was certainly reaping the consequences of her unbridled behavior.

The apostle Paul taught that our bodies are "the temple of God" and that "if any man defile the temple of God, him shall God destroy; for the temple of God is holy, which temple ye are" (1 Corinthians 3:16–17). Though our bodies are a priceless gift from our Father, they are nonetheless his, and we have no authority to do with them as we please without facing serious consequences.

This young woman had contracted a disease that could possibly prevent any future pregnancy. Others who are sexually active contract diseases that literally end their lives. This fifteen-year-old was a mother, with no boyfriend, husband, or parent to provide love and support. With the responsibility of one child at home, she was now contemplating adding to her sins by terminating this new pregnancy. She may have thought she was being grown-up and responsible by acting independently, but clearly she had saddled herself with consequences no teenager should ever have to experience. I had a glimpse into her unhappiness when she told me that she wanted to move far away where no one knew her, to start over again as though nothing had ever happened.

Her yearning to run from the consequences of her choices reminded me of something else President Kimball has said: "There is no night so dark, no room so tightly locked, no canyon so closed in, no desert so totally uninhabited that one can find a place to hide from his sins, from himself, or from the Lord" (*The Teachings of Spencer W. Kimball* [1982], 266). Decide now before the temptation comes—for it surely will come—to be chaste. That decision will bring you true freedom and a happiness beyond anything you can now imagine. Your soul depends upon that decision!

TAKE CONTROL OF YOUR THOUGHTS

The second suggestion is that you take control of your thoughts. A deed is never committed without having thought about it first. No bank was ever robbed without a plan, no virtue ever lost without first allowing thoughts to roam freely where they ought not to go. We cannot separate our thoughts from who we are; they are what define our character. The scriptures teach, "For as he thinketh in his heart, so is he" (Proverbs 23:7). Our thoughts are an intensely personal, private part of us. At any one moment, no one but the Lord can know our inner thoughts, unless we choose to divulge them. How ironic it is that our behavior, something that is available for everyone to see, is a sum of our inner thoughts.

President Gordon B. Hinckley related an experience he had while working for the railroad when a rail car intended for the East Coast ended up in Louisiana. Upon investigation it was discovered that when the train reached St. Louis, a switchman had moved a tiny switch plate to the wrong position. A seemingly small mistake took the train thousands of miles off course (see Conference Report, Oct. 1972, 106–7).

There are many switch plates in our minds, the position of which will determine our behavior and consequently our eternal destination. For some, the switch plate might be activated by the decision to view an inappropriate movie. We have been counseled by our prophets not to see R-rated movies. "Don't see R-rated movies or vulgar videos or participate in any entertainment that is immoral, suggestive, or pornographic" (Ezra Taft Benson, *Ensign,* May 1986, 45). The standard is clear, the Lord doesn't want us to see the images in those movies.

For others, the switch plate to inappropriate thoughts is activated by pornography. Experiences with pornography generally begin with curiosity; however, it rarely stays at that level. Much like alcohol or drugs, pornography first entices, then intoxicates, and finally enslaves. Of particular danger in our day is the computer and the Internet. In the privacy of your room there is the potential to access material that could quickly destroy your soul. Making the temptation more enticing is the mistaken notion that no one will ever know of your sin. Be assured that He who knows you best, knows where you are and what you are doing. Over the past several years in general conferences, apostles and prophets have warned us of the dangers of pornography.

Elder Russell M. Nelson of the Quorum of the Twelve Apostles taught, "Hence, I warn against pornography. It is degrading of women. It is evil. It is infectious, destructive, and addictive. The body has means by which it can cleanse itself from harmful effects of contaminated food or drink. But it cannot vomit back the poison of pornography. Once recorded, it always remains subject to recall, flashing its perverted images across your mind, with power to draw you away from the wholesome things in life. Avoid it like the plague!" (*Ensign,* May 1999, 39).

The switch plate in your mind may be activated by movies, magazines, the Internet, or something we haven't talked about. It may be something that seems simple or even innocent to you. John Wesley, the great religious reformer, received wise counsel from his mother when she said, "Whatever weakens your reason, impairs the tenderness of your conscience, obscures your sense of God, takes off your relish for spiritual things, whatever increases the authority of the body over the mind, that thing is sin to you, however innocent it may seem in itself" (quoted by Ezra Taft Benson, in Conference Report, Oct. 1964, 59). Be careful to position the switch plates of your mind properly; a small misalignment could put you eternally off course.

Even though you might not be consciously aware of your thoughts throughout the day, they are there, from the moment you wake up until the time you drift off to sleep—influencing your decisions, shaping your behavior. How do we control them? I have found that an idle mind is indeed the devil's workshop. If I am able to continually fill my mind with thoughts that build and strengthen my resolve to do what is right, there is much less room for inappropriate thoughts to creep in. It takes a great deal of effort to maintain control of one's thoughts. President Boyd K. Packer has suggested we recite a previously memorized Church hymn to divert bad thoughts. That can be a valuable help when thoughts start to wander.

I have also found it useful to focus on some intensely spiritual experience I have had. I often find myself thinking about an EFY fireside or testimony meeting. I replay the event over and over in my mind to the point where I can almost feel what I was feeling when I was actually there. Quickly, thoughts rise to a more spiritual plane, and I find my heart filled with newly found resolve to do (and to think) what is right.

PRAY FOR POWER TO RESIST TEMPTATION

The third suggestion would be to pray for the power to resist temptation. "Pray always, that you may come off conqueror; yea, that you may conquer Satan, and that you may escape the hands of the servants of Satan that do uphold his work" (D&C 10:5). We should approach our Heavenly Father every day asking for the strength to resist and pleading for the help to position ourselves in places where Satan won't be able to be successful in tempting us. When you feel yourself slipping, when it seems you can't resist temptation any longer, remember the promise given in the New Testament that the Lord will not ever allow us to be tempted beyond our capacity to resist and that he will also provide a way that we can escape the temptation (see 1 Corinthians 10:13). However, it would be a mistake to assume that the promised help will be ours without any effort on our part.

BE PROACTIVE IN RESISTING TEMPTATION

Adhering to a few tried and tested dating habits will help you find the power to stay worthy and clean. One of the most important things you can do to claim the promised blessing of strength from the Lord is to plan and participate in positive, constructive activities or dates. That is not to say that every date needs to be straight out of a manual for creative dating, but it is important that each date be planned well enough that you don't find yourself scrambling for something to do at the last minute. Idle or down-time provides Satan with the opportunity to present his own plans for your date.

It is also true that there is safety in numbers. Elder Boyd K. Packer has counseled, "Stay in group activities. Don't pair off. Avoid steady dating. The right time to begin a courtship is when you have emerged from your teens"(in Conference Report, Apr. 1965, 71). When to begin dating is one of the most important decisions you will make. The Lord's standard on this is also very clear: "Do not date until you are sixteen years old" (*For the Strength of Youth,* 7). Early dating is a time to make new friendships and to have fun. It is not the time to look for an eternal partner. There will be plenty of time for that search when you return from your mission.

Who you date is equally important as *when* you begin dating. Church leaders have counseled us that we should date neither members nor nonmembers who are "untrained and faithless" (Spencer W. Kimball, *The Miracle of Forgiveness* [1969], 241). You must take special care that those you choose to spend time with are those who love the Lord and are determined to live up to his standards—friends who will in turn help you do the same. Let your parents help you with your dating habits. Though it may seem strange to even consider it, your parents have dealt with many of the same dating concerns you now face. "Now, I speak very plainly to you, my young friends. If you are old enough to date, you are old enough to know that your parents have not only the right but the sacred obligation, and they are under counsel from the leaders of the Church to concern themselves with your dating habits" (Boyd K. Packer, in Conference Report, Apr. 1965, 70).

The themes of many movies, the lyrics of many popular songs, the jokes of many prime-time television shows, and even the topic of many high school conversations center on one of the most precious gifts our Heavenly Father has given us: human intimacy. Elder Jeffrey R. Holland summed up a powerful sermon on personal purity by stating: "You and I—who can make neither mountain nor moonlight, not one raindrop or a single rose—have this greater gift in an absolutely unlimited way. And the only control placed on us is self-control. . . . Surely God's trust in us to respect this future-forming gift is an awesomely staggering one. We who may not be able to repair a bicycle or assemble an average jigsaw puzzle can yet, in all of our weaknesses and imperfections, carry this procreative power which makes us so very much like God in at least one grand and majestic way" (*On Earth As It Is in Heaven* [1989], 196).

One day in the not too distant future, you likely will be blessed to kneel across from your marriage partner at a temple altar. Dressed in white, with your sweetheart's hand in yours, you will listen while one with priesthood authority seals you together for eternity. Upon that union will be sealed blessings and promises, which are so glorious as almost to be beyond anyone's ability to comprehend. Your eyes will meet as sacred covenants are made in the presence of God, family, and friends, and then you will know the fullness of joy that being morally clean makes possible. You will understand what President

Kimball meant when he said, "Even mortal life itself, when placed upon the balance scales, weighs less [than chastity]" (*The Teachings of Spencer W. Kimball* [1982], 265).

Curtis Galke is an emergency room and family physician in Blackfoot, Idaho. After graduating from Brigham Young University, he attended medical school in California and then completed a three-year family practice residency with the U.S. Air Force. Upon completion of his residency, Curt and his family lived for three years in Panama, where he worked as a flight surgeon. The highlights of his life include flying in an F-16 fighter jet, playing the Tabernacle organ, serving a mission to Mexico City, and his marriage in the temple. Curtis and his wife, Alethea, and their four sons are eagerly acticipating the birth of their first daughter (and sister).

7

FIGHTING FEAR WITH PRAYER AND FAITH

Cindy Grace

I have to admit that I was a little bit disappointed the first time I actually saw the Sea of Galilee. Because of what it says in the scriptures about the raucous storms and high winds that often occur there, I had imagined it to be a much larger body of water. So when I finally arrived at its shores, my first thought was, "It seems too little to ever get terribly stormy." However, a few days later, while I was at my kibbutz, sitting in the trailer where I was living, a storm suddenly came up. The wind began blowing so hard that it shook the trailer violently. I looked out the window to find that the placid, peaceful sea that I had observed when I first arrived had been transformed into a choppy mass of dark waves. I later learned that being so far below sea level, the lake and the surrounding land is normally very hot. When cold winds come rushing down from the hills and collide with the warmer air, sudden and frequently violent storms do indeed result.

The scriptures were coming to life for me, and I was able to better imagine what Peter had experienced so long ago. Attempting to cross the Sea of Galilee in a small boat in the middle of the night, he and some of the other disciples were caught in one of those sudden storms. At a point where they feared their boat would capsize and they would be drowned, Jesus approached them, walking on the water. Understandably, they were confused and frightened, but the Savior comforted them by saying, "Be of good cheer; it is I; be not afraid" (Matthew 14:27).

Impetuous Peter responded, saying: "Lord, if it be thou, bid me come unto thee on the water" (v. 28). Doubtless extending his hand, Jesus responded simply: "Come" (v. 29). Remarkably, Peter then stepped out of the boat and was able for a moment to himself walk on the water. But feeling the boisterous wind and seeing the turbulent water beneath his feet, Peter lost his courage (and his faith) and began to sink. As he cried out, "Lord, save me," Jesus "stretched forth his hand, and caught him, and said unto him, O thou of little faith, wherefore didst thou doubt?" (vv. 30–31). Peter's faith was strong until he was seized by fear. Faith and fear are actually opposite principles and cannot coexist.

FEAR

Isn't it ironic that fear beset Peter right after the Savior had counseled the disciples not to be afraid? But, losing his focus, perhaps taking his eyes off the Savior to look at the elements swirling around him, Peter became fearful and was unable to continue walking forward. That is true for us as well. When we focus on the storms in our lives rather than on Christ, we are in danger of losing the will to continue moving forward and of spiritually sinking. Fear breeds doubt, and doubt is the opposite of faith, which is required to continue moving forward.

The fact that Peter was so close to the Savior when he sank reminds me of the swimmer Florence Chadwick, who was to be one of the first people ever to swim the English Channel. In one of her earlier, failed attempts, with thick fog obscuring the shore she was about to reach, she gave up just two hundred yards from completing the swim.

I like to think of eternal salvation as our goal or shore. However, it is often hard to keep this eternal perspective when all we can see around us is fog. Let's face it, life can be very discouraging. The evening news is filled with all kinds of tragedy and human suffering, and each of us experiences a certain amount of physical, emotional, or spiritual difficulty in our own lives. These things can obscure our eternal goal, and if they consume us, they'll keep us from moving toward Christ.

It's important to remember that there are two kinds of fear mentioned in the scriptures. One is the "fear of the Lord" or "godly fear." This refers to the reverence and worshipful feelings we should have for our Father in Heaven and for the Savior, Jesus Christ. While "godly fear" moves us toward our Father in Heaven and the Savior, there is a second type of fear, which is to literally be afraid of the Father and the Son. This kind of fear results from sin, which causes us to lose confidence in our relationship with a loving Father in Heaven, and instead, feel shame and guilt. Ever since Adam first transgressed, "God has been teaching men not to fear, but with penitence to ask forgiveness in full confidence of receiving it" (Bible Dictionary, s. v. Fear, 672).

It makes me so sad to hear youth say: "I am afraid that because of my sins, I'm not worthy enough to pray to Heavenly Father." That is exactly how Satan wants us to feel, and when we feel this way is precisely the time we need to get on our knees and ask forgiveness of a loving Father, who wants us to come to him, not in fear, but in confidence and faith.

PRAYER

Like Peter, when we are having difficulty staying afloat spiritually, physically, or emotionally, we too can cry out to our Savior, "Lord, save me" (Matthew 14:30). Remember what happened? "And *immediately* Jesus stretched forth his hand, and caught him" (v. 31; emphasis added). When we pray in faith, believing that God can send his Spirit, we can *immediately* be comforted. Though our prayers ultimately may not be answered in the way that we would choose, we have access, through our faithful prayers, to prompt comfort and spiritual strength.

My two-year-old daughter has begun using a phrase that, although truthful, can be annoying. Any time she does not get her way, she puts her hands on her hips, puts on her best pout, and declares, "It's not fair!" She is learning at a young age that life truly is not fair, but what she can't understand yet is that it's not supposed to be. If life were always perfectly fair, we would lose our opportunity to be tried, tested, and proven worthy to return to our heavenly home someday.

Each of us will experience storms in our lives. None of us is exempt. In fact, Elder Richard G. Scott of the Quorum of the Twelve Apostles has counseled: "You are here on earth for a divine purpose. It is not to be endlessly entertained or to be constantly in full pursuit of pleasure. You are here to be tried, to prove yourself so that you can receive the additional blessings God has for you" (*Ensign,* May 1996, 25). The trials are a necessary part of our growth and refinement here on earth, and with the help of the Lord, we can keep ourselves from becoming consumed by the fear and bitterness that cause so many to go into a downward spiral rather than to move forward. If our trials cannot be taken away, then we can ask for strength to get through them in a way that will allow us to continue progressing forward rather than becoming terribly weighed down by the emotions that accompany trial.

I ran into a friend at the temple who shared some personal fears she had been experiencing due to a recent trial in her life. At the end of our conversation she said, "I have finally realized that I just have to have faith and keep moving forward." She is a wise person. This year's Especially for Youth theme, "Forward with Faith," holds that same kernel of wisdom. In order to move forward, you must replace fear with faith.

FAITH

Faith is a principle of action. Cultivating faith takes work, and for some, even a change of heart. Speaking about how to increase our faith in the Savior, Sister Chieko Okazaki, formerly a member of the General Relief Society

Presidency, used an analogy originally communicated by Helen Keller. Sister Okazaki pointed out that you can see your own shadow only when you turn away from the sun. She further suggested that, if in our lives we are seeing mostly shadows, then we need to make a change because we are facing the wrong direction. We must turn around and face the Son—the Son of God. By concentrating on the Savior, we will focus less on the shadows in our lives and be able also to help illuminate others by our own example of faith (from personal notes taken in a meeting of the South Salt Lake and Granite Park Stakes, Oct. 1999).

Faith in the Savior can be strengthened by hearing the testimony of others. It can be confirmed, but not gained, by hearing of or experiencing miracles. The only way faith may be originally gained is through righteousness—through obedience to the gospel principles and commandments (see Bible Dictionary, s. v. Faith, 669). If you want to know how strong your faith is, ask yourself how obedient you are. Your faith will be in direct proportion to your righteousness and diligence.

The Book of Mormon helps us understand the relationship between obedience, faith, and miracles. Because of his obedience, Nephi's faith in Jesus Christ was so strong that he had angels minister to him daily, and it was impossible for the people to disbelieve his words. Not only that, but Nephi performed many miracles in the sight of the people, such as casting out devils and even raising his brother from the dead after he had been stoned. These miracles kindled anger in the people rather than faith because they would not hearken to the word of the Lord and leave their sins and become obedient. In fact, very few were converted to the Lord. This shows that you don't need miracles to produce strong faith. Nephi gained his iron faith by obedience long before he used it to perform miracles (see 3 Nephi 7:18–21).

If you feel that you are lacking faith, pray for help. The scriptures tell us that even a *desire* to believe, coupled with prayer and obedience, will increase our faith (see Alma 32:27). Next, begin acting upon the word of the Lord. Study the scriptures to learn the things the Savior would have you do, and then actually do them. Follow the counsel of our Church leaders at both the general and local levels. Turn away from fear, sin, anger, and sadness. Turn toward the Son of God and watch the shadows disappear. It may happen slowly or in steps. That's okay. Many of the above emotions are a normal part of our earthly existence, but they should not consume us and thwart our progress. As we call upon the Lord in prayer, and increase our obedience, our faith will become more dominant than the other emotions that grip us during trying times. Such faith will help us keep our focus on the Savior rather than on the storm and will allow us at the end of our course to reach our eternal shore.

As the year 2000 approached, there was much speculation and fear associated with the coming of the new millennium. Fearing computer glitches, people were afraid to fly, leave their money in their bank accounts, or trust in the continuing availability of food, water, or other vital services. Some were even afraid that the earth would spontaneously combust on New Year's Day. Looking back, such fears seem foolish.

In reality we ought to be excited to be living at this time in the world's history, when there will come so many wonderful developments. In his October 1999 general conference address, President Gordon B. Hinckley expressed his faith and made this stirring declaration: "We stand on the summit of the ages, awed by a great and solemn sense of history. This is the last and final dispensation toward which all in the past has pointed. . . . Let the old year go. Let the new year come. Let another century pass. Let a new one take its place. Say good-bye to a millennium. Greet the beginning of another thousand years" (*Ensign,* Nov. 1999, 74). I love President Hinckley's optimistic attitude. He is always looking forward to the glorious possibilities that await us rather than the glitches that often accompany change.

Similarly, we should look forward to the possibility of our Savior's return with gladness for the blessings it will bring rather than with fear for the calamities that will accompany it. In his same conference address, President Hinckley quoted these lines from a favorite hymn:

Come, O thou King of Kings!
We've waited long for thee,
With healing in thy wings,
To set thy people free.
Come, thou desire of nations, come;
Let Israel now be gathered home.
(Hymns, No. 59)

We understand that no man knows the time of the Second Coming, however, if we are to follow our prophet, then shouldn't we also ask for our Savior to return? Should we not also say, "We've waited long"?

As I listened to our prophet give this powerful testimony during the general conference broadcast, my leaky valve struck. Seeing my tears, my daughter, Katie, came to my lap and said, "Oh, Mommy, you sad because you miss your friends?"

At first, I smiled at her childlike misunderstanding of the reason for my tears. Then what she said really struck me, and I said, "Yes, Katie, I miss my friend, and I want to see Him again."

I hope that we will invite Jesus into our lives now, that we will focus on *him* more than on our obstacles, and that we will call on his name in prayer and gain faith through obedience to his word. I testify if we do these things, then we will one day be able to move forward with faith and greet him, not with fear, but with confidence, humility, and joy.

Cindy Grace was born in Rochester, New York, and reared in Sandy, Utah. She served a service mission in Nauvoo, Illinois. After graduating from Brigham Young University with a bachelor's degree in Communications Education, she served as an English teacher at Oak Canyon Junior High and as an adjunct faculty member at BYU. She loves traveling with her husband, Jeff, and singing and reading to her super-social three-year-old, Katie.

8

THE MIRACLE OF FORGIVENESS

Bruce W. Hansen

On several occasions I have begun a class by saying to the students: "When we die and are judged, we will have a bright recollection of all our ________."

Each time the two most frequent responses are "guilt" and "sins." I am grateful for one other possible response, which is significantly more encouraging. Jacob taught that, at the time of judgment, "we shall have a perfect knowledge of all our guilt, and our uncleanness, and our nakedness [don't stop reading yet!]; *and the **righteous** shall have a perfect knowledge of their enjoyment, and their righteousness, being clothed with purity, yea, even with the robe of righteousness"* (2 Nephi 9:14; emphasis added).

The Prophet Joseph Smith taught that "happiness is the object and design of our existence; and will be the end thereof, if we pursue the path that leads to it" (*Teachings of the Prophet Joseph Smith,* 255). Most teenagers have memorized 2 Nephi 2:25 (its length may have something to do with that!), but perhaps some have not pondered the reality that "men are, that they might have *joy"* (emphasis added). The doctrine of the Church is that joy is to be obtained only through purity and righteousness (see Mosiah 4:3, 20; emphasis added).

What about the times in your life when you're not feeling that joy? What hope is there that if you sin (i.e., lie, steal, lose your temper, break the law of chastity), the guilt can be made to go away? To understand the hope offered by the gospel of Jesus Christ and to regain the joy and peace it affords, here are three key points in our Father's plan to consider:

1. We lived in premortal life as literal spirit children of our Heavenly Father. The proclamation on the family teaches, "All human beings—male and female—are created in the image of God. Each is a beloved spirit son or daughter of heavenly parents, and, as such, each has a divine nature and destiny" (*Ensign,* Nov. 1995, 102).

2. While living with Heavenly Father as his sons and daughters prior to your mortal birth you made promises or covenants. President Spencer W. Kimball stated: "Here (referring to the pre-earth life) you and I made . . . an oath that we would do all things whatsoever the Lord our God shall command us. While we do not remember the details, we made these covenants. We committed ourselves to our Heavenly Father that if he would send us to earth and give us bodies and give to us the priceless opportunities that earth life afforded, we would keep our lives clean and would marry in the holy temple and rear a family and teach them righteousness. This was a solemn oath, a solemn promise, an eternal commitment" ("Be Ye Therefore Perfect," an address given at the [University of Utah] Institute of Religion, 10 January 1975).

3. In mortality, you again entered into a covenant relationship with God (i.e., you promised to do your best to be like Jesus). Most of you made such a promise when you were eight years old. Before entering the refreshing waters of baptism you probably memorized the fourth article of faith, where we are reminded that two of the first principles of the gospel are "faith in the Lord Jesus Christ" and "repentance." The repentance part is not as significant for an eight-year-old because he or she is just entering into the age of accountability (see D&C 29:47; 68:25–27). But an eighteen-year-old, on the other hand, greatly anticipates being cleansed of his or her sins, as well as joining the true Church of God. The point is that repentance is as much a part of the Lord's plan as is baptism! President David O. McKay taught: "Every principle and ordinance of the gospel of Jesus Christ is significant and important in contributing to the progress, happiness, and eternal life of man; but there is none more essential to the salvation of the human family than the divine and eternally operative principle, repentance. Without it, no one can be saved. Without it, no one can even progress" (*Improvement Era,* Nov. 1968, 64).

Repentance is not only important with respect to very serious, moral sins, it is a process that should be a part of our everyday life. One may already be involved in this ongoing process and not realize it. Elder Richard L. Evans taught: "Repentance is part of the process of progress, of learning, of maturing, of recognizing law, of recognizing results; it is a process of facing facts. Every correcting of a mistake is a kind of repentance; every sincere apology is a kind of repentance; every improvement is a kind of repentance; every conquering of an unhealthful habit" (*Improvement Era,* Jan. 1965, 43).

Speaking to the young women of the Church, President Gordon B. Hinckley gave this counsel: "Your lives are ahead, and they can be filled with happiness, even though the past may have been marred by sin. This is a work of saving and assisting people with their problems. This is the purpose of the gospel. . . . This is the time, this is the very hour, to *repent* of any evil in the past, to ask for forgiveness, to stand a little taller and then to go forward with confidence and faith" (*Ensign,* May 1996, 94; emphasis added).

You need to remember that just because repentance is always available to you, it doesn't mean you can say, "Eat, drink, and be merry, for tomorrow I go on my mission" (Glenn L. Pace, *Spiritual Revival* [1993], 105). Because of this attitude, many young men never make it into the mission field. Some who have willfully sinned and then attempted to practice "easy repentance" have entered missionary service but not been as effective as they might have been had they always put the Lord first in their lives.

Speaking in general conference, Elder Richard J. Maynes remarked: "If those [teenage] years are fractured with sin and go unrepaired, then the structure of your life will be built upon a weakened foundation. Your future will be less secure and certainly more stressful. . . . Young friends, it is very difficult to cram for a mission, and it is equally difficult to cram for a temple marriage. Don't take the risk. Be wise. Prepare yourselves daily. Study the scriptures. Communicate with your Heavenly Father in prayer. Attend seminary. Keep yourselves clean and prepared. Understand that what happens on Friday night will ultimately impact your celestial future.

"If these seemingly little things seem tiresome, tedious, or time-consuming, carry on! The little things that confound the wise also confound Satan. Remember, celestial blessings are on their way" (*Ensign,* Nov. 1997, 31).

Satan doesn't like the principle of repentance. He only wants you to focus on the here and now, for he has nothing to offer you beyond this life (see 3 Nephi 27:11). That is why all the behavior he sponsors (immorality, stealing, breaking the Word of Wisdom, etc.) offers only a temporary thrill. Nothing Satan encourages results in lasting satisfaction or joy. On the other hand, in return for obedience, the Lord holds out the promise of unimaginable happiness and eternal glory (see 1 Corinthians 2:9).

Whenever you ponder where you came from, why you are here, and where you are going, Satan loses his power and influence over you. For example, those who gave their allegiance to Satan during the war in heaven will never receive a body and never receive any glory. Does that make you want to follow him? It is well to remember that those who reject the gospel and follow instead the devil in mortality have no hope of an eternal family or celestial glory!

The commandments the Lord gives are not meant to restrict you but to prepare you to eventually receive the fullness of God's work and glory. In the October 1999 general conference, Sister Patricia P. Pinegar gave a wonderful example to illustrate the role the commandments play in our lives:

"I enjoyed telling [the full-time missionaries at the MTC] the story of the little boy who went to the park with his father to fly a kite.

"The boy was very young. It was his first experience with kite flying. His father helped him, and after several attempts the kite was in the air. The boy ran and let out more string, and soon the kite was flying high. The little boy was so excited; the kite was beautiful. Eventually there was no more string left to allow the kite to go higher. The boy said to his father, 'Daddy, let's cut the string and let the kite go; I want to see it go higher and higher.'

"His father said, 'Son, the kite won't go higher if we cut the string.'

"'Yes, it will,' responded the little boy. 'The string is holding the kite down; I can feel it.' The father handed a pocketknife to his son. The boy cut the string. In a matter of seconds the kite was out of control. It darted here and there and finally landed in a broken heap. That was difficult for the boy to understand. He felt certain the string was holding the kite down.

"The commandments and laws of God are like the kite string. They lead us and guide us upward. Obedience to these laws gives us peace, hope, and direction" (*Ensign,* Nov. 1999, 67–68).

In an article entitled "Bridle All Your Passions," Bruce C. Hafen and his wife, Marie K. Hafen, warned us about the danger of wanting blessings and gratification from worldly things right now instead of patiently and faithfully waiting for the eternal blessings of the Lord:

"Our family once watched a segment of the children's

television program *Sesame Street* in which the Cookie Monster won a quiz show. What a moment it was! After Mrs. Monster joined her spouse on the stage, the emcee congratulated the couple and offered them their choice among three big prizes—a $200,000 dream home next month, a $20,000 new car next week, or a cookie right now. Mr. and Mrs. Monster furrowed their furry brows and carefully weighed the pros and cons. As the timer buzzed, a big smile broke across Mr. Monster's face, and he greedily announced his choice: 'Cookie!'

"Now, there is nothing wrong with a good cookie. The problem is not that the cookie is bad, but that its satisfaction *cannot last.* Not *should* not, or *might* not, but *cannot* last. Yet, whether the subject is love, education, or investing scarce resources, Satan deludes us into believing that a cookie is more valuable than a dream home—because we can have it right now. His manipulation is full of irony, because *his* long-term intent is that 'all men might be miserable like unto himself.' (2 Ne. 2:27)" (*Ensign,* Feb. 1994, 16).

To avoid being miserable like Satan, all of us need to take advantage of the principle of repentance. When I served as a bishop, I found the following five steps were generally useful in assisting a person to obtain forgiveness:

Experiencing **S**orrow for sin. (Coming to a point where you feel that you have offended God by your actions.)

Abandoning the sin. (Finding the will to leave the sinful actions and change your behavior.)

Confessing the sin. (First to the Lord and then to the bishop and those you might have offended or hurt.)

Making **R**estitution. (Repairing the damage your sinful behavior might have caused, to the extent this is possible.)

Resolving to **D**o the will of the Lord. (See Elder Spencer W. Kimball, "Be Ye Clean," in *Speeches of the Year, 1954* [1955], 8–9).

The acronym **SACReD** (a word formed from the first

letter or group of letters of words in a set phrase) will help remind you of the steps involved in the repentance process.

The reason I said these principles are "generally useful" is that an individual may still not have experienced the "miracle of forgiveness," despite having worked his or her way through these steps. The scriptures teach us that true repentance is accompanied by a "mighty change of heart" (see Mosiah 5:2; 27:25; Alma 5:12–14, 26; Helaman 15:7; to name a few). The Bible Dictionary says that "repentance comes to mean a turning of the heart and will to God and a renunciation of sin to which we are naturally inclined. Without this there can be no progress in the things of the soul's salvation, for all accountable persons are stained by sin, and must be cleansed in order to enter the kingdom of heaven. Repentance is not optional for salvation; it is a commandment of God" (s. v. Repentance, 760–61).

Many years ago a young person, who had previously repented, made an appointment to see me in my bishop's office. After some small talk, I asked the reason for the appointment, and she said, "No reason in particular. I just wanted to see what it was like having an appointment when I had no sins to confess!" If this young woman felt the joy of seeing her bishop when she felt clean and pure, imagine the ultimate joy of having her "confidence wax strong in the presence of God" (D&C 121:45).

I testify that we are members of the true Church of Jesus Christ. He made the ultimate sacrifice so that we could receive his greatest gift—eternal life (see D&C 14:7). The Spirit promised to you in both sacrament prayers is the same cleansing Spirit that was confirmed upon you after your baptism. In other words, if you have truly repented of any wrongdoing, you are as clean and pure after worthily partaking of the sacrament as you were the day you were baptized!

When speaking at the funeral of a young child, Joseph Smith admonished a large gathering of Saints near the

Nauvoo Temple: "We should take warning and not wait for the deathbed to repent, as we see the infant taken away by death, so may youth and middle aged, as well as the infant, be suddenly called into eternity. Let this, then, prove as a warning to all not to procrastinate repentance, or wait till a deathbed for it is the will of God that man should repent and serve Him in health, and in the strength and power of his mind, in order to secure His blessing, and not wait until he is called to die" (*Teachings of the Prophet Joseph Smith,* 197).

Before burying the gold plates, the prophet Moroni testified of the cleansing power of the Atonement of Jesus Christ: "And again, if ye by the grace of God are perfect in Christ, and deny not his power, then are ye sanctified in Christ by the grace of God, through the shedding of the blood of Christ, which is in the covenant of the Father unto the remission of your sins, that ye become holy, without spot" (Moroni 10:33).

We will all stand before Jesus Christ at the judgment bar (see 2 Nephi 9:15, 22, 38). Rather than have a bright recollection of all our sins and guilt, wouldn't it be wonderful to have a perfect knowledge of our enjoyments and righteousness? I testify that this "miracle of forgiveness" is possible because of the love and mercy of our Lord and Savior, Jesus Christ.

Bruce W. Hansen is an instructor at the Las Vegas Institute of Religion. He has been teaching for the Church Educational System for seventeen years and has been an EFY speaker since 1989. Bruce holds a master's degree in Counseling and Educational Psychology. He served a mission in Frankfurt, Germany, while his future wife was serving in Paris, France. Brother Hansen has been a bishop and is currently a member of the stake high council. He enjoys playing Ping-Pong at the institute and basketball anywhere. Bruce and his wife, Leanne, have five children.

9

"I STAND AT THE DOOR AND KNOCK"

Daniel Hess

One night, just after midnight, I found myself at our local 24-hour grocery store picking up milk and some training pants for my youngest daughter. I walked down the aisle through the infant section with its bottles and formula, past the endless varieties of baby foods and teething rings, beyond the toddler toys until I was finally in front of the "little girl" shelf. As I was deciding between the cuddly kitten and Miss Piggy design, I felt a heaviness in my heart that accompanies the all-too-frequent realization that my baby is growing up. How I longed to be able to go back to the other end of the aisle and begin all over again.

To make things worse, on my way home, "Butterfly Kisses" (a song about a father and his daughter who is growing up) was playing on the radio. While the tears came to my eyes, which is nothing new when I hear that song, I found myself pleading with Heavenly Father for the safety, health, and happiness of my daughters. I promised him that I would do whatever it took to be the best dad I can be.

In the pale light of early morning, I love to stand in the doorway of their bedrooms and look at their beautiful faces as they sleep. I almost always smile, but there are occasions when I frown, remembering that my girls continue to break their promise to me—the promise that they will stop growing up.

I love my daughters with all that I have and am. Next to their beautiful mother, Janalee, they are the most important people in my life. There is nothing that is within my power that I wouldn't do for them. But I realize that power is limited. As much as I love my girls, I will never be able to save them. I will never cleanse them from their sins or exalt them on high. But there is Someone who can and will do those things for them, and the greatest thing I could ever do for my girls is to help them learn to love and desire to come to Him.

During quiet moments, I have often felt the overwhelming peace and love of my Heavenly Father reassure me, as if to say, "Dan, don't worry. Long before they were your girls, they were mine. And as much as you love them, I love them even more and have provided a way for them to come home." That love and direction is not restricted to my girls. Heavenly Father loves you with a love such as we cannot comprehend right now. A love which allowed him to send his Only Begotten Son to suffer, bleed, and die so that you might come home someday. This is not a passive love nor is it love from a distance. Your Heavenly Father and your Savior Jesus Christ want so much to be a part of your life. They long, perhaps even ache, to be included in every aspect and moment of your day. In fact, Jesus has assured us, "Behold, I stand at the door, and knock: if any man hear my voice, and open the door, I will come in to him, and will sup with him, and he with me" (Revelation 3:20).

You have probably seen an artist's rendition of this scene—the Savior standing and knocking at a door. What do you notice about the outside of the door? There is no doorknob, no handle, no latches. Nothing to provide access from the outside. The Savior stands *waiting*. He will not open your door and come marching uninvited into your life, proclaiming, "Here I am! I'll fix this and I'll take care of that. My, it's a good thing I came when I did."

No, it's you, from within, who must open the door. You are the one who must invite Christ into your life and into your heart. And, my friend, if your life is anything like mine, the Savior is doing a whole lot more than politely tapping. I imagine that there is some urgency: "Dan, I'm right here. I've got so many things that I want you to see, so many things that I want you to feel and experience and know. But I can't do that until you let me. Please let me in. Please, let me in."

I promise. He's there. The moment you open your door, Jesus will come in.

After delivering what we call the Sermon on the Mount, as Jesus came down from the mountain into the streets of the city, he met a man afflicted with leprosy: "And, behold, there came a leper and worshipped him, saying, Lord, if thou wilt, thou canst make me clean" (Matthew 8:2). Did you notice the way the man worded his request? He did not say, "if thou *canst*." There was no doubt, no uncertainty that Christ *could* make him clean. The only question was whether or not Jesus *would* make him clean.

I love the Savior's response, because I know it is the same response that he will give to you when you reach out to him and invite his healing influence and power into your life. In verse three it says, "And Jesus put forth his hand, and touched him, saying, I will; be thou clean. And immediately his leprosy was cleansed." Once you open the door, Jesus will touch you. He will heal you.

As you think about the Savior entering, perhaps you will remember some things in your life that don't belong there, things that need to be taken out or cleaned up. Hopefully, you won't be ashamed that he is there. Rather, you'll realize that the purpose of his visit is to help you rid yourself of such things. That is why he comes to us. He wishes to lift and bless us, and as you invite him to do so, his response will be: "I will!" And he'll take you by the hand, saying, "Let's begin! Let's not wait another moment. Let's go!" Just as Alma the younger did, you will feel joy as exquisite as was your pain. You will be made clean (see Alma 36).

Then you will notice that Jesus has not left. He remains with you because he wants to be a part of your whole life and not just pieces of it. I think we sometimes limit what Christ can do and be in our lives because we mistakenly believe that the Atonement is limited—that there are some things it doesn't cover or can't make right. If we believe that his atoning sacrifice has to do only with forgiving our sins, we do not fully understand. And though I testify with all my heart that Jesus paid the penalty for our sins and that he can and will forgive us, I also testify that there is so much more.

What about the pain, sorrow, and struggles we experience because of something other than sin? Isn't that suffering just as real? Have you ever felt lonely, discouraged, depressed? What about the grief that comes with the death of a loved one or the sorrow over a friend who has fallen away from the truth? Aren't those afflictions and so many others just as painful to endure? Who is going to relieve that suffering and heal those wounds? It is the same One who cleanses us from sin.

Alma understood these things very well, and he taught: "And [Christ] shall go forth, suffering *pains* and *afflictions* and *temptations* of *every* kind; and this that the word might be fulfilled which saith he will take upon him the *pains* and the *sicknesses* of his people. And he will take upon him death, that he may loose the bands of death which bind his people; and he will take upon him their *infirmities,* that his bowels may be filled with mercy, *according to the flesh,* that he may know *according to the flesh* how to succor his people according to their *infirmities*" (Alma 7:11–12; emphasis added).

Have you ever shared the innermost thoughts and feelings of your heart with someone and had them respond by saying something like, "I know how you feel. I've been there"? And even though it may have been said with all the love and concern in the world, perhaps you've thought, *I don't know that you do. I don't know if anyone really knows how I feel.* Well, I would simply share that there *is* someone who knows *exactly* how you feel because he *has* been there, and that is your Lord and Savior Jesus Christ. There is nothing that you will ever think, feel, or experience that Jesus has not already experienced. There is nothing beyond his understanding or that exceeds his desire and power to heal you and make you whole. The question is not: "Can he or will he heal me?" The question is: "Will I allow him to heal me?"

Let's go back to the book of Matthew, this time to chapter 14. Here, the Savior miraculously feeds several thousand people, and while he is sending the multitude away, his disciples are following his instructions to enter into their ship on the sea. Then "he went up into a mountain apart to pray: and when the evening was come, he was there alone" (v. 23). Now I don't know how you feel about it, but I love the fact that even Jesus Christ, the Son of God, occasionally needed some time to be alone with his Father. And if that is true for him, what about you? Do you ever feel the need to just get away from everyone and everything and open up your heart and soul to your Heavenly Father? I know your Father longs for those moments with you.

"But the ship was now in the midst of the sea, tossed with waves: for the wind was contrary. And in the fourth watch of the night Jesus went unto them, walking on the sea" (vv. 24–25). The scriptures don't reveal how long the storm had been raging, but remember that when the evening was come, at roughly 6:00 P.M., the disciples were already in their ship, and that it is now the fourth watch of the night (check your footnotes to discover that it is between three and six in the morning). Is it possible that they had been battling this storm for maybe eight, ten, even up to twelve hours? Wouldn't they be weary, worried, afraid even for their very lives? Does that sound a little like your life sometimes? Whatever storms mortality or the adversary would have you pass through, even those that will push you to the very limit, Jesus will always be there. Don't forget, he's been through the same storm before. Remember what the Lord said to Joseph Smith while the Prophet was in Liberty Jail: "All these things shall give thee experience, and shall be for thy good. The Son of Man hath descended below them all. Art thou greater than he?"(D&C 122:7–8).

"And when the disciples saw him walking on the sea, they were troubled, saying, It is a spirit; and they cried out for fear" (Matthew 14:26). Do your fears keep you from opening your door? How do you overcome and conquer them? Writing to Timothy, the apostle Paul said, "God hath not given us the spirit of fear; but of power, and of love, and of a sound mind. Be not thou therefore ashamed of the testimony of our Lord" (2 Timothy 1:7–8). If God doesn't give us the spirit of fear, it's easy to discern who does. Our prophet, President Gordon B. Hinckley, has admonished us concerning Paul's words, "I wish that every member of this church would put those words where he might see them every morning as he begins his day. They would give us the courage to speak up, they would give us the faith to try, they would strengthen our conviction of the Lord Jesus Christ. I believe that more miracles would happen over the earth" (*Ensign,* Feb. 1996, 5).

Could you use some more miracles? Follow the prophet. Study and ponder what President Hinckley has said to the youth of the Church since becoming our president. If there was ever a time in the world's history that needed a clear voice in the midst of chaos, that time is now, and President Hinckley is that voice. Don't be deceived by counterfeit invitations that offer everything and then only deliver momentary pleasure followed by misery and captivity. Don't let Satan and fear keep you from opening your door and experiencing the miracle that is Christ.

Imagine yourself in the boat with the disciples and listen: "But straightway Jesus spake unto them, saying, Be of good cheer; it is I; be not afraid. And Peter answered him and said, Lord, if it be thou, bid me come unto thee on the water. And he said, Come" (Matthew 14:27–29). Oh, my friend, isn't that exactly what Jesus is saying to you every day of your life? His invitation calls to you: "Come unto me, all ye that labour and are heavy laden, and I will give you rest. Take my yoke upon you, and learn of me; for I am meek and lowly in heart: and ye shall find rest unto your souls. For my yoke is easy, and my burden is light" (Matthew 11:28–30).

The Savior doesn't invite you to come and follow him as he is walking away. He does so as he wraps you in the arms of his love and walks beside you. Elder Jeffrey R. Holland has testified: "The Savior of the world will walk that essential journey with you. He will strengthen you when you waver. He will be your light when it seems most dark. He will take your hand and be your hope when hope seems all you have left. His compassion and mercy, with all their cleansing power, are freely given (*Ensign,* Nov. 1998, 78).

"And when Peter was come down out of the ship, he walked on the water, to go to Jesus. But when he saw the wind boisterous, he was afraid" (Matthew 14:29–30). It's at this point in the story that Peter begins to sink into the water. Unfortunately, some people hold up what happened to him as an example of Peter's lack of faith. I don't see it that way. First of all, Peter got out of the boat! No one else did that. Secondly, Peter actually walks on the water! Other than the Savior, no one else was able to do so. Sure, he begins to sink, but who doesn't? Even if you are as focused as Peter and you're moving toward Jesus, there will be those times in your life when all you can see are the waves and all you can hear is the storm. It is in those moments that your faith, like a shaft of light, shines through. Not just faith, but faith in the Lord Jesus Christ.

Consider what Peter does (this is my favorite part!). "And beginning to sink, he cried, saying, Lord, save me" (v. 30). I love that! I love Peter! He realized that he was in trouble, and he knew that alone he couldn't fix it. Notice that Peter does not say, "Lord, don't touch me! I can fix this—just give me a minute." Rather, Peter looked to the source of his salvation and cried, "Lord, save me," and "*immediately* Jesus stretched forth his hand, and caught him" (v. 31; emphasis added). Now I don't mean to say that the moment you invite Christ into your life that *immediately* all of your problems will vanish or that *immediately* all of your doubts will disappear or that *immediately* your questions will be answered. But what I do say is that the moment you invite Jesus in, *immediately* he will touch you and *immediately* he will begin to raise you up. I know it!

So how do you invite Christ in? How do you open your door? Well, the Lord has taught us that it is the Spirit that will teach us all things that we should do (see D&C 75:10). So put yourself in an environment where the Spirit can be comfortable. Find one of those quiet moments, as Christ did, and pray to your Father in Heaven. Share everything with him. I mean, everything! There is absolutely nothing in your life that is trivial or unimportant to Heavenly Father. As a dad, I know for myself that is true. You are his child, formed in his image, with the potential to become even as he is and inherit all that he has to give. You are his work and his glory. Please allow Father in Heaven to work for you and be glorified in you. Let him truly be your father.

Be aware that there will be opposition. The last thing Satan wants is for you to call upon your Father and open your door to your Savior. Don't let the evil one win. Pray, listen, ponder, feel, understand, and then have the faith and courage to obey what the Spirit tells you to do. Remember, the Lord is bound to bless us when we do what he says, but when we do not what he says, we have no promise, and he remains closed out (see D&C 82:10).

Perhaps the way you open the door to him is by getting on your knees at least every morning and night. Your door could be the cover of your scriptures, which, when opened, will reveal a whole new world with the Savior right in the center. Even if you begin by reading just one verse a day and open the door just a crack, guess whom you will see waiting, knocking, hoping? If you continue, pretty soon that door will be wide open. Your door could lead into your seminary classroom or your chapel or maybe your bishop's office. As you open each of these doors you are answering the Savior's knock and inviting him to come in.

Just as I am observing my daughters growing up, your Heavenly Father looks at you at this very moment and sees his child growing up—a child whom he loves more than you know. A child whom he misses. A child whom he wants to come home and be with him forever. A child to whom he has given the gift of his Only Begotten Son. Do you hear the knocking?

I end with my answer to the question posed by those who sat at meat with Jesus and wondered, "Who is this that forgiveth sins also?" I testify he is Jehovah. He is the promised Messiah. He is Jesus Christ, the literal Son of our

Father in Heaven. He is my Lord, my God, my Savior, my best friend. He stands at your door and knocks. Please, let him in. Please, let him in.

Daniel Hess was born in Salt Lake City and served a full-time mission in the Philippine Islands. While attending Brigham Young University, he worked as a trainer at the Missionary Training Center in Provo, Utah. He graduated with a degree in Theatre and Film and has also received his master's degree in Theatre and Media Arts.

Daniel is married to the love of his life, the former Janalee Williams, and they are the parents of four daughters: Cassandra, Julia, Ashlee, and Savannah. Brother Hess teaches seminary and institute at the Timpview Seminary in Provo, Utah, and has been associated with Youth and Family Programs through BYU since 1989. He loves teaching, acting, sports, being involved with the youth of the Church, and most of all, being a husband and a daddy.

10

THE SERMON ON THE MOUNT: WHAT DOES IT MEAN FOR ME?

Curtis L. Jacobs

Some time ago, I happened to see a notice on a bulletin board in the hall of a church. It read: "Going to church no more makes you a good Christian, than living in a garage makes you a car."

At first I thought, what? But the more I considered what it was saying, the more I realized it was true. Attending our meetings is certainly important, but that alone may simply make us an active member of the Church, not necessarily a good one.

So, what makes a good member or a good Christian? Some would say, "Well, we don't drink or smoke, we don't fool around, we read our scriptures, we say our prayers, and we certainly go to church a lot." All of these answers would be true, but there's more to it.

If you look up the word *Christian* in the dictionary, you'll find a fairly easy definition. A Christian is "a believer in Jesus as the Christ or in the religion based on the teachings of Jesus, . . . *having the qualities taught by Jesus*" (Webster's *New World Dictionary;* emphasis added).

Jesus himself said, "Not every one that saith unto me, Lord, Lord, shall enter into the kingdom of heaven; but he that doeth the will of my Father which is in heaven" (Matthew 7:21).

Notice, we must do the will of Heavenly Father. If you were to go back to the time Christ lived on the earth and ask the Jewish people what the will of God is, they would probably refer you to the Law of Moses. You know, the Ten Commandments, certain sacrifices, and ancient rites, etc. However, in his sermon on the mount, Christ taught a higher law than the Law of Moses. Some have referred to it as the Law of Christ.

Take a look at Matthew 5, beginning with verse 21. Notice that Jesus begins by saying, "Ye have heard that it was said by them of old time, Thou shalt not kill . . ." You've heard that, right? Killing is one of the Big 10, and you probably have it marked in Exodus 20:13. After all, it is a scripture mastery reference. Now, I'm making a big assumption that very few of you have ever actually killed someone. Sure, maybe the thought crossed your mind when your little brother or sister just got you in trouble or when your best friend began to date the guy or girl you'd been working on for the past year. But let's be real, none of us actually went through with what we were thinking.

However, Christ didn't stop at, "It was said by them of old time. . . ." He added, "But I say unto you, That whosoever is angry with his brother without a cause [the Book of Mormon takes out the phrase "without a cause"] shall be in danger of the judgment" (Matthew 5:22). Now, how many of us have maybe, say, just once (or twice, or three times, okay, probably lots of times) been angry with our brother (or sister, or friend, or parent, or . . . ? Well, you get the point). Likely most of us.

Why isn't it okay to get angry, especially if I don't actually punch out the person I'm angry with? If you think about it, part of the reason we are here on earth is to see if we can control ourselves, and that doesn't mean just our actions. King Benjamin warns us: "If [we] do not watch [our]selves, and [our] thoughts, and [our] words, and [our] deeds," we are in danger of falling into sin (Mosiah 4:30). It's not easy to control our thoughts or our words, but it can be done. It's obvious that if we are able to control our words and thoughts when it comes to getting angry, we'll never have to worry about killing someone.

Let's consider another teaching from the Sermon on the Mount. Christ again refers to the Old Testament: "Ye have heard that it was said by them of old time, Thou shalt not commit adultery." (Yes, that's another of the Ten Commandments.) "But I say unto you, That whosever looketh on a woman to lust after her hath committed adultery with her already in his heart" (Matthew 5:27–28). Now, which is harder, not committing adultery (or fornication for that matter) or not even thinking about it? Once again the Lord is trying to get us to control our thoughts. But how in the world, especially the world in which we live, can you never "lust"?

Everywhere you go it seems, there are pictures, movies, videos, magazines, etc., that entice us to have unworthy, unclean thoughts. I once talked with a recently returned missionary who came to me as his bishop for a temple recommend. He was a fine young man. He told me about one area of his mission that made it really hard to keep his thoughts clean. I asked him what he meant. He told me that one day as he and his companion were headed for their area, right in front of him on the side of a building was a picture several stories high that was completely inappropriate. He quickly stopped looking at it and looked down, only to see that someone had plastered the sidewalk with more pornography. "What's a missionary supposed to do?" he asked.

First, let's understand what the Savior did *not* say. He did not say it's the same thing to think about adultery as it is to actually commit adultery. I've known a few young people who have mistakenly felt that if they were having these kinds of thoughts they might as well go ahead, since it's just as bad. No, while bad enough, it's not the same.

Second, let's define a phrase he mentioned. "Lust after her." What does that mean? Can a young man or woman look at a member of the opposite sex and think, *Oh, he's a babe* or *She's really cute* and not be lusting? Sure. But, if you find yourself thinking thoughts that you know you wouldn't want your parents or bishop to know about, then you'd better start working on changing what you're thinking about.

Be careful not to go places where you really (in your heart) know there will be some form of pornography. Be careful in your dating. Don't think you won't be tempted, because chances are in time you will. Discipline yourself to leave any situation if necessary.

The Savior also challenges us to live a higher law with regard to keeping our word. He says, "Again, ye have heard that it hath been said by them of old time, Thou shalt not forswear thyself [i.e., break your oath, or in today's vernacular, your promise or word], but shalt perform unto the Lord thine oaths" (Matthew 5:33). Now that's not one of the "Big 10," but the idea is found in Deuteronomy 23:21. In today's business world, people agree to something and then generally have a contract written up. Unfortunately, many people seem to be unable to abide by such agreements. For instance, I love all types of sports, but I'm not impressed with an athlete who signs a contract for say, three years, and then, at the end of the first or second year, decides he's not making enough money, and holds out until they make him a better offer. Didn't he agree beforehand what he'd make? Doesn't his word mean *anything?* Compare that attitude with one expressed by Karl G. Maeser, who said, "Place me behind prison walls, walls of stone ever so thick, reaching ever so far into the ground, there is a possibility that in some way or another I may be able to escape; but stand me on the floor and draw a chalk line around me and have me give my word of honor never to cross it. Can I ever get out of that circle? No, never! I'd die first" (*BYU Speeches of the Year, 1960* [1961],21).

The higher law is: "But let your communication be, Yea, yea; Nay, nay" (Matthew 5:37). I remember teaching my children this years ago. Afterward, one of my sons went around all day saying, "Yea, yea, nay, nay." I don't think that is what the Savior means. Let's put it this way, if you say, "Yes, I'll do that," or "No, I won't do that," then your word should be your bond. People who are known to keep their word are far more easily trusted. As we try to make our way through life, to be trusted is a benefit all of us can use.

Ready for another? The Savior says, "Ye have heard that it hath been said, An eye for an eye, and a tooth for a tooth" (Matthew 5:38). Now, I know a few high school guys who love that statement. It's called "getting even." But Christ desires us to be better than that: "But I say unto you, That ye resist not evil [i.e., against you], but whosoever shall smite thee on thy right cheek, turn to him the other also" (see Matthew 5:39). Some of you may be thinking, *But that would make me look like a wimp!*

Just a minute. Was Christ a wimp? When he was unjustly accused, spit upon, and beaten, he could have responded by calling down angels from heaven to avenge him (Matthew 26:53), but he didn't. Can we all follow his example by trying a little harder to act with the same kind of restraint?

The Savior tells us, "Judge not unrighteously, that ye be not judged; but judge righteous judgment" (JST Matthew 7:2; see also John 7:24). I know that if I'm not careful I find myself judging others wrongfully. Once a lady came to me at the end of an institute class I was teaching. She looked very unkempt, her hair really needed some help, her mouth looked a little funny, and she certainly wasn't up-to-date in the fashion world. My first thought was, *Why doesn't she do something about the way she looks?*

As we chatted in my office, she sadly informed me that she couldn't continue the class. When I asked her why not, she told me that some months before, they'd found a tumor by her brain, which she had had removed. The surgery resulted in her almost entirely losing the sight in one eye. The doctor had told her to be careful reading, etc. Then she mentioned the surgery had caused her mouth to hang down a little and that as a result of her poor health, her hair would never be the same. She didn't like her appearance but couldn't really do much about it.

By the time she left my office, I was feeling pretty humble. I couldn't believe I had been so unfeeling and so willing to jump to a conclusion. I had been entirely wrong about her and wondered how I could have made such a judgment. I have tried ever since to be careful not to judge so quickly.

Have you noticed how some young people seem to judge everyone around them? They can't seem to keep their mouth shut, unless it's to say something mean. The Lord warned, "For with what judgment ye judge, ye shall be judged: and with what measure ye mete, it shall be measured to you again" (Matthew 7:2).

My wife and I recently had the opportunity to be on the northeastern coast of the United States in the beautiful state of Maine. We were impressed by the number of picturesque lighthouses that dot the rocky shores of that state. They can be seen for miles away, and they warn passing ships of the dangerous shallows and rocky outcroppings. We drove right up to one, and there, with the powerful waves rolling in from the Atlantic Ocean, it stood firm and unshaken. You could see the surf pounding against the cliff and hear the roar of the waves, but the lighthouse was unaffected.

The sturdy lighthouses reminded me of the Savior's closing words in his marvelous sermon:

"Therefore whosoever heareth these sayings of mine, and doeth them, I will liken him unto a wise man, which built his house upon a rock:

"And the rain descended, and the floods came, and the winds blew, and beat upon that house; and it fell not: for it was founded upon a rock.

"And every one that heareth these sayings of mine, and doeth them not, shall be likened unto a foolish man, which built his house upon the sand:

"And the rain descended, and the floods came, and the winds blew, and beat upon that house; and it fell: and great was the fall of it" (Matthew 7:24–27).

I have to ask myself, am I building my eternal house on sand or on the rock? It's probably a lot easier at first to build a house on sand, but it won't last when the going gets tough. Building a house on rock is harder. Sure, not getting angry or not lusting after someone or always keeping your word or being careful not to judge wrongfully isn't always easy, but in the long run, those who choose to follow the Savior will still have a house, a strong house, a beautiful house, and one that can stand forever.

Curtis L. Jacobs has worked for the Church Educational System programs since 1979 and with the Especially for Youth program since 1984. Brother Jacobs has taught seminary and institute in Arizona and has spent the last few years teaching at Utah State University. He and his wife, Jolene, are the parents of four very active children. Curtis is a raquetball fanatic and loves Les Misérables.

11

SPEAKING OF SPEECHES

Allen Litchfield

Have you noticed how during 1999 the media busied itself compiling lists of the greatest this and that? Among such lists were those naming the greatest statesmen, events, movies, actors, songs, and athletes of the past. Reading these lists has been entertaining, and they have ignited a lot of debate. As I have read or heard some of those discussions, I have found it amusing that some expert thinks he or she can distinguish between the fifth or sixth best movie or linebacker of the decade or century.

If such debates have any value, I suppose it is that they recognize and perhaps promote excellence. With that in mind, I would like to propose a list of my own—of the best speeches of all time. You may have others you would include, but these are some of my all-time favorites.

As a school child, I remember being told by my teachers that Patrick Henry's 1775 speech given in Virginia, the one that ended with the memorable declaration "Give me liberty or give me death," was the best of an era. My special favorite, though, from the early years of our nation's history was Abraham Lincoln's 1863 Gettysburg's Address that began with "Four score and seven years ago" and concluded with his ringing definition of democracy.

I have a friend who is an avid baseball fan, who claims

that, though the sound system created a distracting echo, the moving farewell speech given by Lou Gehrig in 1939 in Yankee Stadium was the best speech ever given by an athlete. That was the speech in which, though he was dying, Lou Gehrig said that because he was a Yankee and so widely loved, he considered himself "the luckiest man in the world."

During the dark days of World War II, my parents were moved by the encouraging speeches given by U.S. President Franklin D. Roosevelt and British Prime Minister Sir Winston Churchill—particularly Churchill's "This was their finest hour" radio message given in 1940.

But my own personal memory is dominated by two outstanding political speeches. In January 1961, a young President John F. Kennedy delivered his inaugural address to the nation. We were all touched by his stirring call to "Ask not what your country can do for you but ask rather what you can do for your country." Two years later, in 1963, Dr. Martin Luther King Jr. stood on the steps at the Lincoln Memorial and delivered his inspiring "I have a dream" speech, which was presented to America on the hundredth anniversary of the previously mentioned Gettysburg Address. Listening to that declaration of hope, in which Dr. King defined his vision of America, still gives me goosebumps. These are powerful and beautiful messages, which moved me and everyone who heard them.

There have been many marvelous speeches given over the years by LDS Church leaders in general conferences and other settings. Among those I recall personally hearing was the one given in April 1976 by Elder Boyd K. Packer, who used the analogy of crocodiles that lie unseen in muddy water holes, waiting to attack and kill unsuspecting zebra, wildebeest, or antelope. No one who heard that powerful talk will ever forget the warning Elder Packer gave about avoiding "spiritual crocodiles," and his speech has impacted a whole generation of youth.

President Ezra Taft Benson's landmark sermon, given in October 1989 and warning the Saints to beware of pride, continues to be widely quoted and have an impact in the lives of the Saints. President Gordon B. Hinckley has given many outstanding sermons. His presentation on "The Family: A Proclamation to the World," given in a General Relief Society Meeting in September of 1995, will be a great beacon not only to the Church but to the world for decades. We are blessed to be able to hear these messages and study them. Why don't you track down some of these talks in the back issues of the *Ensign* magazine and enjoy them again?

These famous historical and LDS addresses are among the most influential speeches that I am aware of, but I believe they all pale in comparison to the greatest speech ever given. I humbly suggest that the Sermon on the Mount, delivered by the Savior to the disciples in Galilee and later to the people of the Book of Mormon lands, is the greatest speech that we have any record of. Each idea or phrase within this speech is a sermon by itself and, in fact, has been the text of hundreds of sermons since. This speech continues to challenge and change lives two millennia after its delivery.

The sermon is found in chapters 5, 6, and 7 of the book of Matthew in the New Testament. I suggest that you get out your Bible and do some marking of these chapters as you read this article. In chapter 5, the Savior invites the disciples to transcend the superficial interpretations of the requirements of the Law of Moses and live a higher law. Jesus explained that murder was wicked, but that we ought to avoid, in addition, the very roots of violence and hostility toward others. He went on to say that adultery was wrong, but that we should also avoid the lascivious thoughts that create feelings of lust and lead to immoral behavior. The Savior also asked his followers to go the extra mile and to love even their enemies. Finally, he challenged them to "Be ye therefore perfect, even as your Father which is in heaven is perfect" (Matthew 5:48).

Building on that higher law foundation, the Savior discussed, in what is now chapter 6 of Matthew, three fundamentals of Christian living that must be central to our faith—the giving of alms, prayer, and fasting.

Jesus did not for a moment dismiss or even diminish these religious practices in his sermon. This is a very important point because some critics of religion have seen hypocrisy in the observance of these religious practices and concluded that charitable giving, prayer, and fasting should be abandoned. Sometimes critics even propose that religion is irrelevant because some people practice it hypocritically. Interestingly, those same people might admit that some educational, political, and theatrical performances are also fraught with hypocrisy, yet few of them are calling for an end to schools, the government, and entertainment. One of my dear friends came to the mistaken conclusion that he couldn't be involved in the LDS Church anymore because some Church members are hypocrites.

Jesus acknowledged that men often act insincerely but condemned the practice. In his profound sermon, Jesus called upon his followers to avoid hypocrisy. He condemned outward, showy demonstrations of righteousness and said of those who perform their religious rites to be admired of men, "Verily I say unto you, They have their reward" (Matthew 6:16). The Savior also commanded us not to perform our charitable acts for the "glory of men" (v. 2). And he stated that praying to "be seen of men" is an empty and pointless exercise (v. 5). Finally, he stated that fasting to "appear unto men to fast" is of no spiritual value (v. 16). Notice again that the Savior never even hinted that these practices weren't important or worthwhile. Instead, he taught that the way they were being done prevented the insincere worshiper from tapping into the powers of heaven and obtaining the promised blessings.

In the Sermon on the Mount, Jesus offers a spiritual model to his disciples that provides enormous delight, power, and the Spirit through charitable activity, prayer, and fasting. Giving alms as the hypocrites do (to obtain acclaim) only makes one poorer, in time and/or money. Giving alms the Savior's way makes one richer. Praying in the manner of the hypocrite results in detachment, boredom, and dissatisfaction, while preventing the individual from tapping into the benefits of prayer. Praying as the Savior taught empowers and invigorates a person and fills him or her with the Holy Spirit. Fasting in the manner of the hypocrite only results in physical hunger and weakness, while fasting as the Savior prescribes, energizes and invigorates a person and fills him or her with joy.

Consider the following analogy. Some people don't really enjoy exercising, even if they know they should. Exercise, done improperly, can leave one simply tired, sore, and frustrated. Watch people come out of a health spa or the gym and notice that some seem absolutely beaten. Now, some of those people who view exercise as torture will come back and do it again because they know that it is good for them. But done right, exercise can invigorate and energize and still provide the health benefits. That is why some people leave the spa almost doing cartwheels—they literally bounce out the door, smiling, laughing, and brimming with energy. Like a skilled personal trainer, Jesus coaches us in his sermon to do alms, pray, and fast in a way that is enjoyable and will also allow us to harvest the great spiritual blessings he delights to give us.

THE GIVING OF ALMS

The first religious practice the Lord discusses is the doing of or giving of alms, which originally meant the giving of money or commodities to the poor, but in the Savior's sermon probably represents the performance of any charitable service toward others. In the parable of the good Samaritan, the act of giving alms went far beyond dropping a few coins in a cup. The charitable person not only went out of his way to provide immediate care but took responsibility for the future welfare of the unfortunate victim. In encouraging us to behave kindly, Jesus asks that we perform such acts in secret. Instead of sounding a trumpet, which would be like calling a news conference whenever we were about to do something generous in the world of today, the Lord asks us to serve quietly and without fanfare. To emphasize this he provided us this striking image: "But when thou doest alms, let not thy left hand know what thy right hand doeth" (Matthew 6:3).

There is something spiritually thrilling about doing nice things for people when no one ever discovers who did it. May I give some examples of secret service? Some of my own children's favorite memories are of doing Secret Santa or Twelve Days of Christmas or Pixie surprises for people who to this day don't know who dropped stuff in ingenious ways at their door. A man in my stake supported a young man, who was a recent convert, for the entire two years of his mission. The young man wanted very much to know whom his benefactor was so that he could thank him directly, but the kind giver refused to allow his name to ever be revealed. He wanted all the thanks to go to the Lord, whom he said inspired his generosity and provided him with all the rewards he desired.

While I was serving as bishop, we heard a few weeks in advance that a Latter-day Saint refugee family from Central America was being moved into our area. The bishop where they had been temporarily housed informed me that they had nothing except two small suitcases of clothing. We rented them an unfurnished apartment and announced to the ward that ward members could borrow the keys to the apartment from the bishopric to look around the modest place to see if there was anything they might donate or fix up to make it more inviting. Over the two weeks before the family arrived, repairs, painting, and cleaning were all provided anonymously. Furniture, clothing, food, really everything they would need to get started, magically arrived. The day we moved the family into their apartment they found the refrigerator stocked, flowers on the table, sheets and pillows on the beds, a crib and toys for the baby. They asked who had done all this for them. We just said that many great friends who loved them but hadn't met them yet had been involved. The ward just sparkled with love and happiness during this period because they had been involved in giving alms in the spirit of Matthew 6. In Acts 20:35, Paul explains why we were so happy, by quoting the Savior's teaching that "It is more blessed to give than to receive." I testify that providing anonymous charitable service results in happiness and brings great spiritual blessings.

PRAYER

The second religious practice analyzed in the sermon is prayer. Prayer and charity actually go together as Amulek explained in his sermon to the Zoramites. He taught that if we pray mightily and then turn away the needy, neglect the sick, or fail to impart of our substance to the poor, we are "as hypocrites who do deny the faith" (Alma 34:28). Mormon, quoted by his son Moroni, establishes the same connection. He defines and describes charity and then encourages us to "pray unto the Father with all the energy of heart, that ye may be filled with this love [charity]" (Moroni 7:48). In addition to linking prayer and charity, Mormon also describes the higher and most effective kind of prayers, ones that are uttered with "all the energy of heart." These prayers are not necessarily long, eloquent, or filled with poetic language, but rather are heartfelt, honest, and humble.

We understand that the Lord hears every prayer, but it seems he responds most directly to communications actually aimed his way. Prayers that are spoken in the interest of a social performance are not really intended to go up to God. Such prayers are calculated to bring the person performing the prayer acclaim, recognition, and honor. The Lord seems to be telling us that long, pompous, showy prayers do not let the person praying really connect with him. Prayers uttered in this spirit are prayers to men or, in other words, idolatry. The Lord hopes that we will not settle for such a short-term reward as the praise of men and so asks that we not use "vain repetitions" and "much speaking" in our prayers (Matthew 6:7). He wants us to pray in a meaningful way because that is the way we communicate with God, and he wants to hear from us—*really* hear from us. In Luke 18:9–14, Jesus compares and contrasts two prayers—the showy, insincere prayer of the Pharisee with the humble, submissive supplication of the despised publican. The prayer of the Pharisee was to himself or other men, so that is where the prayer went, while the publican's prayer actually created a link to God and having uttered it, the man "went down to his house justified" (Luke 18:14).

Because we as Church members are often called upon to pray publicly, we can get into a rut with our prayers and sometimes merely rattle off something filled with clichés and trite phrases. Hurried prayers, such as those uttered over meals during commercial breaks on television, are sometimes not really thought out. This is especially true of prayers that are said routinely— such as blessings on the food and opening prayers offered in seminary.

The Lord set the example of meaningful prayer and specifically asked us to follow it (see 3 Nephi 18:16). The night before he called twelve of his disciples to serve as apostles, "he went out into a mountain to pray, and continued all night in prayer to God" (Luke 6:12). In the Sermon on the Mount, Jesus uttered the beautiful prayer we sometimes call the Lord's Prayer (see Matthew 6:9–13).

During his night of agony in the Garden of Gethsemane, "he prayed more earnestly" (Luke 22:44). He prayed with such power during his visitation to the Book of Mormon peoples that having witnessed that prayer, Nephi testified "The eye hath never seen, neither hath the ear heard, before, so great and marvelous things as we saw and heard Jesus speak unto the Father" (3 Nephi 17:16).

Just because we cannot pray at that level doesn't mean we shouldn't at least follow the model that Jesus provided us. May I also suggest that if you haven't sincerely prayed for some time that you try praying out loud in your "closet" or some other quiet place where you will be undisturbed (3 Nephi 13:6). Some people who have strayed from the habit of praying find it easier to concentrate when they pray vocally. I testify that praying earnestly and with real intent is the way to access spiritual blessings. James says it this way: "The effectual fervent prayer of a righteous man availeth much" (James 5:16).

FASTING

Finally, Jesus discusses the blessings associated with fasting. Years ago in a class for young married couples that my wife and I were attending, the teacher made the following statement, "If you don't like kissing, then you are not doing it right." I believe that is what the scriptures are trying to teach us about fasting: if you don't like fasting, you are not doing it right! Though fasting involves going without food, if that is all you do, you will just end up hungry. It is clear from D&C 59:13–14 that fasting is related to joy and rejoicing. Zechariah 8:19 reminds us that fasting has to do with joy and gladness. Helaman 3:35 suggests that fasting makes one stronger. If we are not experiencing that spiritual joy and strength as a result of our fasting, then we are probably not fasting, but simply skipping meals. Remember that time you got out of bed late and dashed off to school without breakfast? Then at lunch you had no money or no time, so you skipped lunch, too. Were you really fasting that day or just missing meals? As a small child on fast Sunday, I would sometimes open the refrigerator door. My mom had special powers God gives mothers and could somehow hear the refrigerator light come on even though she was all the way downstairs. She would call out, "Close the fridge, we are fasting." The point is that *we* weren't fasting. Only *she* was fasting; I was merely being deprived of food. Later on in my life, I discovered that fasting involves much more than missing meals.

Esther understood the power that comes with real fasting. When her people were threatened with extermination, and she was the only hope for Israel, she asked that all the people fast with her (see Esther 4:16). She wasn't thinking that skipping meals for three days would somehow work a miracle, but she knew that fasting is the way we demonstrate our faith while imploring God to grant us a blessing. The Lord has given us the fast to help us be worthy of his grace and generosity. Remember that fasting is a spiritual exercise that happens to involve abstaining from food. But it is not the same as starving.

Notice that the king in the story of Daniel in the lion's den "passed the night fasting: neither were instruments of musick brought before him: and his sleep went from him" (Daniel 6:18). Passing the night fasting doesn't sound too difficult because we rarely have meals during the night, except for those midnight pizzas, but the verse suggests that there was more going on than just no midnight snacks that night. The king was focusing on spiritual matters. I am not suggesting that appropriate music or a good night's sleep will destroy the spirit of our fast, but the kind of fasting Jesus recommended clearly involves achieving a spiritual focus. When the psalmist claims that he humbled his soul with fasting (see Psalm 35:13), he was saying that something spiritual happened as he truly fasted. The Pharisee of Luke 18:12 boasted that he fasted twice every week, so he probably missed as many meals as anyone, but he seems never to have tasted the sweet practice of really fasting. I testify that really fasting with focus and purpose brings great spiritual blessings.

I promise you that performing alms, praying, and fasting, done the Lord's way, brings joy and spiritual peace. Remember that if we don't like these activities, we are not doing them right yet. Let us try doing them the way the Lord asks and feel the power of his warm embrace and love. When we do acts of charity, we are doing them unto our God (see Mosiah 2:17; Matthew 25:40). When we pray with real intent, we are communicating directly with our God. When we set aside the things of the world and focus on the things of God as we fast, we are approaching his throne. All three activities are worshipful acts and bring us to him. In his glorious sermon, because he wants us near, Jesus told us how.

Allen Litchfield married Gladys Gough and is the father of six children. He is also a former bishop and district president. Allen is an instructor of religion at Brigham Young University. A former bank administrator, he has served as a seminary teacher and principal and as an institute instructor and director. He enjoys reading, horseback riding, whitewater rafting, and canoeing.

12

SAYING I LOVE YOU

Todd B. Parker

I would like to share with you a very personal experience. The story is true. It is about death. It's about mistakes. Although it is painful for me to recall and uncomfortable to relive, if it can be of help to you then the effort will not have been in vain. My purpose is the same as that expressed in a few words written by Moroni near the end of the Book of Mormon: "Condemn me not because of mine imperfection, . . . but rather give thanks unto God that he hath made manifest unto you [my] imperfections, that ye may learn to be more wise than [I] have been" (Mormon 9:31).

I'd like you to imagine something. Pretend you are at school and that your school principal has called you out of class. He takes you to his office and informs you that your mother (or father, whichever situation suits you best) has been in a serious automobile accident. Your parent is in the intensive care unit at a nearby hospital, lying in a coma. The principal has been instructed to rush you to the hospital. As you mentally travel to the hospital, imagine what you would say to your parent if you knew you could only have two minutes with them before they died.

What *would* you say under those circumstances? Do you have some things you have postponed saying that would be important to share? Consider the last five years of your life. Would you be frustrated by guilt and the recollection of things that you should have communicated but rarely had?

I put you in this position because that is where I found myself. I was sitting in the stairwell of the McKay-Dee Hospital in Ogden, Utah. My mother was in a coma in their intensive care unit, dying. I was crying and praying that she would regain consciousness for at least two final minutes so that I could say some things that were long, long overdue.

If you were suddenly in a position to have only two minutes to spend with one of your parents in mortality, what would you want to say? Would there be some long overdue thank-you's to express? How long has it been since you said, "I love you"?

As I sat in that stairwell alone with my grief and guilt, hiding from my family and friends, I stared out a window at a bleak, gray, frozen world on a dismal January day. With tears in my eyes and a lump in my throat, I searched my memory for the last time I had told my mother that I loved her. To the best of my memory, it was during a Mother's Day program when I was in the third grade. I had stood on a little box and said into the microphone, "Of all the mothers kind and true, you're the best and I love you." I remember my mother's eyes filling with tears, and I wondered if I had said my lines wrong. Third grade! It had been since the third grade! I was then a sophomore in college. How could I have been so selfish, so self-absorbed, and so insensitive to her feelings for so long!

My mind drifted to the past. The memories of what my mother had done for me over the years overwhelmed me. Someone once said, "Help us, O God, to remember that the little things completed are better than the big ones planned." Mom had been so good with the "little things"—little things such as the surprise birthday party and the Howdy Doody puppet she got for me, which I thought I couldn't live without. Little things such as helping me with my paper route on bitter cold January mornings when the snow was knee deep. And other things, such as patiently drilling me on the two hundred most often misspelled words in business letters for my sixth-grade spelling bee. She spent hour after hour working with me. After I won the spelling bee and my friends overdid the celebration by carrying me down the hall on their shoulders, I remember thinking, "They really should be carrying my mom."

To this day, twenty-seven years after it took place, I still have a vivid mental image of the day of my mother's funeral. At the conclusion of the service, those friends of my mine actually *did carry my mom,* but it was as the pallbearers of her casket, to her final resting place in the Ogden City Cemetery.

Mom was always there for me. I remember something she did when I was a sophomore in high school. I was a member of the cross-country running team, and at that time, earning an athletic letter was the most important thing in the world to me. There was an important meet between six or seven schools coming up, and I knew that if I could finish fifth or better in the race, I would earn my letter. I longed to do well and planned to give a superhuman effort in that race, which was to be run after dark before the start of a night football game.

The race began at the mouth of Ogden Canyon and was to end in the football stadium. There were quite a few people at the starting line, but we would run the race with few or no spectators along the way. The real crowd would be in the stadium, waiting to cheer the runners as the race ended. I imagined the conclusion of that race, with the stands full of people acknowledging the runners—cheering for us wildly. It seemed like every year there would be a surprise runner who would finish in the top five. This year, I decided, was my year to be the surprise finisher.

On the evening of the race, just before I left to go up to the high school, my mom said, "Would you like me to pray with you?" It was typical of her to be so thoughtful. I remember that as we knelt at the side of her bed, she prayed that I "might give my best effort" and that "if she could be of help in any way" that the Lord would let her know what it would be.

I was so scared as we lined up to begin. The course was two miles long, and I figured that if I could finish in under ten minutes, I could place in the top five. However, the best time I had ever made for a *single* mile was five minutes, so running two consecutive sub-five-minute miles didn't seem likely. But, part of the course was downhill, which I knew would help. I was determined to do it. My strategy would be to stay with the lead runners for the first mile and then hang on during the second.

After running the first mile, I was exhausted. My legs felt like lead, my arms ached, and my lungs felt like they were ready to burst. I didn't think I could even finish the race, let alone keep up the five-minute-per-mile pace. As I approached the mile and three-quarter mark, my body wanted to quit. I prayed, "Dear God, help me keep going and not collapse. Help me to just keep moving."

Then it happened. I heard a voice. It was my mom's voice. She was standing under the arc light at Fowler Avenue cheering for her son. No other spectators were anywhere near. Everyone else had driven down from the mouth of the canyon to the stadium, where they were waiting to see the finish of the race. But there was Mom, standing all alone in the dark, shouting encouragement to me. She had known. She had known exactly where I would need her and how to inspire me. I can't explain it, but something happened. It was more spiritual than physical. I got a second wind. I looked up. Through the rain that was then falling, I could see three runners ahead of me. I was in fourth place! Something inside of me said, "You can do it—you can hold this pace."

I finished fourth and was awarded a trophy, which qualified me for my cross-country letter and a letter jacket. As I look back now and remember all the things my mother did for me, I realize I owe even my letter to my mom.

Now, the story. I had come home from a track workout at Weber College to find my entire family gathered for dinner. We all had such varied schedules, it was unusual that we would all be together. But Mom had planned it this way. She had some news to share.

"I have an announcement," she said simply. "I am going to have an operation to remove a growth from inside my abdomen. The doctor doesn't know if it's cancerous or not. The test results aren't back yet, but I'm having surgery on January eighteenth." I could tell she was worried. My eyes shifted to my dad. His face reflected the same concern. I guess it was because of my faith in my mother's faith that I didn't worry at first.

One evening prior to the operation, Mom came into my room where I was studying. She said, "I'm worried. Let me show you something." She held my hand and positioned my fingers on her abdomen. I could feel a lump the size of a grapefruit. She said, "This lump has grown so fast it scares me." It wasn't until then that I began to worry.

The next day at church, during Sunday School, a young lady gave a talk in which she read a story entitled "If Only." It was about a young girl who had been very rude to her little brother. Realizing she had been unjustly critical of Timmy and had hurt his feelings, she had planned to make up for her inappropriate behavior and apologize to him after school that day. She never got the chance. During the day Timmy was struck and killed by a car as he was crossing the street to show his mother the model airplane he had made.

Looking back, I now believe that talk was given for my benefit. It made me think: "What if something goes wrong during the operation? What if my mother doesn't make it through this surgery alive? Will I be like the girl in the story, kneeling at a grave staring in disbelief at a headstone and praying for forgiveness? Will I be thinking as the sorrowful girl had, *If only I had two last minutes with him. If only he would ask me again, "Are you mad at me?" I could say, "No, I'm so sorry for the way I treated you. I love you."*

I got this awful feeling of dread about the surgery. I couldn't shake it. I felt as though time was running out, and I knew I had some things I needed to tell my mom—things she needed to hear before going into surgery. I don't know why it had been so hard for me to tell her how I felt about her. After all, it was just three little words, and I really did love my mom, with all my heart. But it had been years since I'd told her so. I wonder now how I could have been so insensitive. I committed to myself that I'd tell her in the morning.

I awoke with a feeling of urgency to tell my mom that I loved her. I realize now, although I didn't then, that it was the Spirit whispering to me. I knew I needed to do it. I went into the kitchen where my mom was fixing breakfast and said, "Uh, Mom."

"What, dear?" she asked.

I heard myself say, "Oh, nothing."

I went back into my room. *Why can't I do this?* I asked myself. *Am I too proud? Do I think this is beneath my dignity? Do I think this is too "mushy"? What's wrong with me?* I muttered to myself, "She needs to hear these words. She deserves to hear them!" So I went back into the kitchen.

"Mom?"

"Yes?"

"Uh, is breakfast ready?"

"In a minute."

Back to my room I went. I couldn't believe myself! I gave myself another mental tongue lashing, another pep talk, and another challenge. I tried again and failed a third time. So I took the coward's way out. I left a note on her pillow containing those three words and left for school.

I came home for lunch to a scene I'll never forget. The house was clean, the laundry done, and the fridge and freezer were filled with things we could easily fix for meals in her absence. She'd had her hair done, and she was typing up my brother's wedding list. I plopped down in a chair and asked for lunch. Did she say, "Could you please fix yourself a sandwich, I'm busy right now." No. Not my mom. She stopped what she was doing and cooked me a hot meal. In the process she cut her finger with a knife while trying to open a package of frozen lima beans. She asked me to help her stop the bleeding. I impatiently interrupted my reading of *Sports Illustrated* to help.

With her finger wrapped in gauze and holding her hand above her heart to slow the bleeding, she fixed the last meal she would ever fix in mortality. It was a meal for a proud, egocentric, selfish, insensitive son who was more caught up in a sports magazine than spending a last few moments with his mother before she left for the hospital. I was oblivious to the possibility that she was leaving home for the last time.

With suitcase in hand, she said to me, "Can I talk to you for a minute?"

"What do you need?" I asked. Then, her eyes brimming with tears, she said, "I got your note this morning. Why is it in this family we can't tell each other we love each other?"

"I don't know," I said, hanging my head. She then added, "I just wanted to tell you, before I left for the hospital, that I love you very much—because I don't know if I will be seeing you tomorrow."

I don't know if she actually meant the next morning before the operation or if she had a premonition of what the future held.

This was my moment. The moment was right. The Spirit was right. But for a fourth time, my pride stood in my way of saying those three little words, and Mom left for the hospital.

The next morning my dad asked me, "Do you want to see Mom in the hospital before she goes in for surgery today?"

I had a big English test that I needed to study for, but I felt a need to see her. "Yeah, I'll come," I told my dad.

As we entered Mom's hospital room, she seemed surprised to see me. She said, "I was hoping you'd come. I have something for you." It was a little quotation she had written out. I collected quotations, and she knew I'd like this particular one. It didn't even occur to me then that I was the one who should be bringing her a gift, but just as they always had, my needs superseded hers.

An orderly came in and prepared Mom's IV. We followed him as he pushed the gurney Mom was lying on toward the operating room. My heart started to pound. I needed to tell her that I loved her. Time was running out. We entered the elevator. She smiled and winked at me. I almost said the words but thought to myself, *There are too many people in the elevator. They might hear me and think it is mushy. I'll tell her when we get off.*

The moment we stepped off the elevator, the orderly quickly pushed the gurney toward the big double doors marked Surgery. Mom looked over her shoulder, smiled, and waved. My heart sickened as she was wheeled away and, with her, my last chance to tell her. I never got the words out. It was like a bad dream where you're trying to speak, but for some inexplicable reason you can't. That was the last time I saw her conscious.

I went home and tried to study but couldn't. After a couple of hours, the phone rang. It was Dad. He was obviously weeping, and he said, "Let me get hold of myself." My heart sank. I thought, "Oh, no. Please, no."

After Dad regained his composure, he said the operation had gone well. They had removed the growth and they were closing the incision when Mom (he paused to compose himself) had gone into cardiac arrest. Her heart stopped. Dad said they had tried several different things and had finally gotten her heart started again. "She's in a coma. She's not breathing for herself. A respirator is breathing for her," came the unbelievable words over the phone. Dad then said, "Call Wendy (my sister) and come up to the intensive care unit on the third floor. I'll meet you there."

I hung up the phone in disbelief. This couldn't be happening. This sort of thing was what I'd always heard about happening to other people, but not to *me,* not to *my* mom.

I called Wendy. It wasn't until I heard her start to cry that the reality started to set in. This wasn't some TV drama that I was watching where I could change the channel and all would be well. This was real.

I drove to the hospital trying to exercise faith that all would be well. Dad met us in the intensive care waiting room. Although his world had just come crashing down around him, he was trying to be strong. He told us only one person was allowed at her bedside at a time. He also said we should try to talk to Mom in an effort to help bring her out of the coma.

When it came my turn to go in and see her, the experience just about killed me. Mom had tubes running down her nose and throat with tape all over her face. Her hair that had looked so pretty hours before was matted down. Attached to her were several wires and tubes leading to various machines. I held her hand and spoke to her. There was no response.

For three days she lingered. Dad refused to go home and literally lived in the waiting room that whole time. The doctor finally persuaded him to go home for some rest. After we drove him home, I remember he mechanically walked into his bedroom but immediately turned around and walked out, into the hallway. He was weeping. "I can't go in there," he said, "all her things are there. It's too painful." Knowing how much he needed rest, I asked, "Will it be okay if I just lie down beside you so we can both try to get some rest?" He agreed.

He didn't sleep, though. I'd doze off and then awaken and look over at him. He would be staring at the ceiling, tears rolling down his cheeks.

At 4:30 the next morning, the phone rang. Dad got up and answered it. I heard him say, "Hello. . . . Yes. . . . Okay." He hung up the phone and slowly shuffled to the doorway of the bedroom. I sat up on the bed. All I could see was the outline of my crestfallen dad silhouetted against the light in the hall. All he said was, "She's gone." Then he collapsed on the bed and began to weep.

I called my brothers and sister, and together we drove Dad to the hospital. We gathered around her bed. Mom looked peaceful. The tubes and tape were gone. The machines were quiet. After a moment, Dad said, "Let's pray." As the family encircled the bed arm in arm, Dad thanked the Lord for the blessing Mom had been to all of us. When the time came for the family to leave, I said, "Go ahead. I'll be there in a minute."

I rearranged the curtains hanging from the ceiling around the bed for privacy. I took my mom by the hand. I wept as I looked at the wound on her finger from the cut she received opening the frozen lima beans. It was then that I realized (bless her heart) that in the concluding day of her conscious life she had shed her blood for me. That was only one of the many ways that her life had been similar to the Savior's.

So, standing in an intensive care unit, holding my mother's lifeless hand, my heart filled with regret, I finally spoke the words. I said, "Mom, I don't know if you can hear me. I'm sorry I've been so proud and so selfish for so long. But I want you to know I love you, and I'm proud to be your son." The words were finally said, but the timing was so very wrong.

I've made a commitment to myself because of this experience. When I enter the next life, the first thing I'm going to do is find my mom. I'm going to do then what I should have done here. I'll embrace her, kiss her, and my first words will be, "Mom, I love you. I've waited so long to tell you."

My challenge to you, my young friends, is don't wait. Don't think it will be easier or that another time will be better to tell your parents that you love them. I know what it's like to miss that opportunity. I agonize over the thought of anyone experiencing anything similar to what I went through.

Fortunately, though, I also know what it's like to take advantage of the opportunity to express my love to a parent. On the Memorial Day after Mom died, Dad and I were standing at her grave site. I looked down at a dual headstone with both of my parents' names engraved on it. My mother was laid to rest there; my father was standing at my side. I thought of those wintry January nights when I had come to that place alone to kneel in the snow and pray. I thought of the opportunity that I had lost. In spite of being warned by the talk I'd heard in Sunday School and being prompted five times by the Spirit, I had still failed to tell Mom I loved her. I thought of the sad task of sorting through Mom's things after her death and finding the note I'd left on her pillow the day she went in for surgery. Then the Spirit whispered to me, "Tell your dad. You've never told him you love him."

So I put my arm around Dad's shoulder, took a deep breath, and said, "Dad, this is hard for me, but I don't want to make the same mistake twice." I tried to say what I wanted to say, but the words caught in my throat just like they had when I tried to say them to my mom. I said to myself, *No! Not* this *time. I won't let this happen again.* I had to force the words, but I managed to say, "Dad, I love you." He cried. I cried. It was one of the most precious and sacred moments of my life. It changed things for me. My relationship with my dad has never been the same.

I began with the words of Moroni. May I conclude with the words of Alma: "Could ye say, if ye were called to die at this time, within yourselves, that ye have been sufficiently humble? . . . Behold, are ye stripped of pride? I say unto you, if ye are not ye are not prepared to meet God" (Alma 5:27–28).

It is my prayer that each of us may examine our lives and remove pride in whatever form we find it. It may be pride in material things such as clothing, cars, or compact discs. It may be pride in less material things such as popularity, athletic ability, intelligence, or social status. It may be for you as it was for me, when I mistook emotion for weakness and wrongly assumed it wasn't masculine to express tender feelings. Whatever may be preventing you from speaking your heart, may you overcome it. I testify that the Lord wants us to set aside our pride and humble ourselves and that when we do, he blesses us with great joy. If that same Spirit that nudged me years ago is now nudging you—respond to it. Don't wait. Tell them.

Todd Parker holds a bachelor's degree in English, a master's degree in Counseling and Guidance, and an Ed.D. in Educational Psychology and is an associate professor of ancient scripture at BYU. Brother Parker served as a seminary teacher for fourteen years and an institute instructor for five years. Maintaining a life-long interest in athletics, Todd remains involved in distance running, pole-vaulting, and soccer. He is married to Debra Harbertson, and they have nine children. He serves as bishop of the Orem Canyon View Fifth Ward in Orem, Utah.

13

PHARISEES, SCRIBES, HYPOCRITES, AND . . .

Kim M. Peterson

It's opening night. You've rehearsed for several weeks. After three years in the chorus line you feel that you deserve to have the lead in your school musical. The costumes are great, the scenery is set, your friends and family are in the audience, and you're just nervous enough to make you perform well. The musical starts without a hitch, and you make it through the first act in perfect form. This is surely going to be your big night.

In the exciting second act, your counterpart is supposed to say, "I love you, and I'll always be true . . ." This line sets up your whole speech about lasting love and the permanence of commitment. The rest of the musical hinges on this theme, and this is the crucial moment. Imagine your surprise if your partner were to look at you with a committed look but blurt out that he or she's reconsidered and thinks that he or she is really in love with someone else.

Those in the audience who know the musical would probably cringe. The director would frantically try to salvage the performance. The orchestra pit might erupt with laughter, but none would be as surprised or confused as you. From that moment on, your lines, your songs, and your performance would cease to have meaning. Everything would be disjointed. Truly the play would become no more than an act, and no more believable than a four-year-old telling a lie.

Think of the plan of salvation as a musical play. Heavenly Father has authored a beautiful script and composed a fabulous musical score, with eternal love serving as the theme. He has created a marvelous set: a world filled with beauty, contrast, and trap doors. He's cast you alongside accomplished actresses and actors and has provided plenty of room for you to show off your talents and abilities. For the climactic finale, he has empowered you with agency and sent a Savior to guide you back to him. With everything all set up and a triumphant completion of your performance within reach, imagine his disappointment were you to depart from the script to go some other direction.

We depart whenever we choose momentary pleasure over eternal joy, when we choose captivity over freedom (see 2 Nephi 2:27), or when we choose wickedness instead of happiness (see Alma 41:10). All these divert us from the script and ruin the structure and outcome of the play. When we begin to improvise and move outside the guidelines, God's profound musical is distorted and turned into a chaotic sideshow.

Diversions lead us into dead ends and create frustration and confusion. For example, consider smoking. Though I've never tried a cigarette, every smoker I've asked has conceded that smoking their first cigarette was actually a miserable experience. If that is true, these smokers became smokers only after *acting* like smokers. They only learned to enjoy smoking after *pretending* to enjoy smoking. Your Heavenly Father didn't create you to be a smoker (or a sinner, for that matter), but you can become one if you choose. By choosing to be a smoker, a liar, a cheater, a fornicator, a disrespectful child, a Sabbath breaker, or a thief, you would be distorting the role you were intended to play—a faithful child of Heavenly Father.

PHARISEES

It is one thing to pretend to be someone or something else when we are performing on stage. But in life, when we pretend to be something other than what we are, that is called hypocrisy—something that Christ condemned when he was on earth.

During his ministry among the Jews, Jesus had many awkward interactions with the Pharisees. The Pharisees were a group of religious zealots who "prided themselves on their strict observance of the law" (Bible Dictionary, s. v. Pharisees, 750). But the Pharisees were guilty of a strange sort of hypocrisy. None could condemn them for disobedience; they always did what was right according to their law. For all their obedience to the law, however, they didn't recognize the lawgiver—Jesus Christ. Interestingly, the outward obedience of the Pharisees was not enough to ensure their salvation. Perhaps they were trying to find some sort of salvation by percentage or degree. While 90 percent may earn you an A in school, 10 percent evil is still too much to gain entrance into the kingdom of God in heaven. Nephi confirmed that "no unclean thing can dwell with God" (1 Nephi 10:21).

My wife, Terri, taught our family this lesson by relating a dream she had. In this dream, she and I were thieves. In her words, "We were nice thieves." Each night we would break into houses, steal old doll clothes (okay, I didn't get that part either), baby high chairs, and other things that we didn't think the people would miss. We never would break windows, make a mess, or destroy property, but we would help ourselves to things we could use (I guess we really had a need for doll clothes at the time). Despite the fact we were thieves, we were nice thieves.

One night the inevitable happened: we got caught. The

lady of the house discovered us rummaging through her things and called the police. Politely, we explained that we were nice thieves and were terribly sorry. By the time the police came, we had even convinced this woman that we were nice thieves, but she still turned us over to the cops. On the ride to the station house, we convinced two arresting officers that we were nice thieves, but they still put us in handcuffs, took our fingerprints, and had us pose for mug shots.

Terri said that when it came time to be put in jail, the seriousness of our crimes finally hit us. We were going to be separated, and it didn't matter whether we were nice people or not! The weight of our guilt was overwhelming, and the thought of separation was unbearable. In reality, we were criminals and were going to jail. You can imagine how relieved my wife was when she realized the awful mess we had gotten ourselves into was only a dream.

Like the nice thieves of Terri's dream, our obedience is imperfect. Interlaced with our successes are occasional mistakes. We mostly obey but partly rebel. One day we will come to understand that every sin is hypocritical, rebellious, and intentional; none of our sins are sincere, submissive, or accidental. As intentional, rebellious hypocrites, we might benefit from asking whether we obey Christ or just commandments. This might be illustrated by the difference between going to church on Sunday and keeping the Sabbath Day holy, or the difference between reluctantly doing what parents say and actually honoring our parents.

Shunning immorality, profanity, vulgar stories, alcohol, cigarettes, and coffee are ultimately only partial evidence of our desire to be clean and pure before the Lord. The psalmist asked: "Who shall ascend into the hill of the Lord?" The answer is: "He that hath clean hands, and a pure heart" (Psalm 24:3–4). If clean hands symbolize our actions and a pure heart symbolizes righteous desires of our hearts, we would have to conclude that both *obedience* and *worthy intentions* are required if we are to return to our Heavenly Father's presence.

Near the end of his mortal ministry, Jesus Christ condemned the Pharisees for cleaning the outside of a cup that contained filthy liquid (see Matthew 23:26). This image vividly describes the activity of appearing to be clean while harboring filth. In the school musical, only the actors who act with feeling are believable. The rest may know their lines, wear the costumes, and enter on cue, but they won't be believable. While it may be better to do the right thing for the wrong reason rather than not do the right thing at all, only doing the right things for the right reasons will replace spiritual hypocrisy with eternal integrity. The Pharisees were good actors. They knew their lines but missed the message of the play. They entered on cue but didn't have a clue. They dressed for their part but were naked before the scrutiny of the Lord. They prided themselves on keeping the law but ultimately crucified the lawgiver.

SCRIBES

Just as he condemned the Pharisees, Christ frequently condemned the scribes. During the time of Christ, a scribe was someone who attempted to interpret the law and apply it to everyday life. Most of the scribes were also Pharisees. As these scribes interpreted the law, traditions and religious observances began to emerge that were conceived of as helps people could use to keep the commandments. Eventually these traditions became more important than the law and superseded the importance of the commandments (see Bible Dictionary, s. v. Scribe, 770). In the school musical, the scribes would be the ones who tell everyone else how to be good actors. They love opening night, publicity, and the cast parties—the trappings of the theater.

It is difficult to be righteous without appearing to be

self-righteous. As soon as others know that you don't drink or smoke or carouse, they might suppose you don't have a sense of humor or are unfriendly and narrow-mined, too. Maybe you've had the experience of trying to explain why you don't drink, smoke, or swear. These can be tense moments filled with anxiety. Why *do* you keep the commandments?

My old dog, Butch, taught me a great lesson in obedience and the reasons for obedience. Butch was a yellow lab. When he was young, I taught him to come to me when I called. At first, I gave him a cookie when he came. Before long, he came just because I called.

One day I was in our neighbor's yard, pruning his tree, and I saw Butch on the other side of the fence sniffing around in our yard. I whistled and called to him. Immediately, his ears perked up, and he came running toward the fence. The laws of physics were against him from the beginning: the fence was six feet high and Butch was only about one and a half feet tall. But he made a valiant attempt to leap the fence, only to slam into the wooden slats and crumple to the ground.

Just for fun, I called him again. Whimpering with excitement, he backed up and made another run at the fence. This time he made it a little higher, but he still missed the mark. I thought two failures would be enough to discourage him, but just for kicks, I called to him again. This time he ran in a circle around our garage and came charging at the fence as though using his momentum as a sort of catapult. He made a mighty leap at the fence and actually managed to hook his front paws on the top of the fence. With his hind feet scratching desperately at the wooden slats, he was able to cling for a moment to the top of the fence. But then, whimpering, he finally fell dejectedly back to the ground.

What motivated my dog to obey? At first, it might have been fear. Maybe he was afraid of being banished to his dog run or chained up for disobedience. Some people obey the Lord out of fear. But fear isn't the best motivation, although the scriptures do say that "the fear of the Lord is the *beginning* of knowledge" (Proverbs 1:7; emphasis added). At some point, don't you think that the fear (and pain) of hitting the fence would have discouraged Butch from trying again? Maybe you know people for whom the fear of getting hurt isn't enough to keep them from playing sports on the Sabbath, or for whom the fear of addiction isn't enough to keep them from trying a drink or a harmful drug.

Perhaps Butch tried again and again to leap the fence because I used to give him a cookie. King Benjamin did teach that when we keep the commandments, God immediately blesses us. Furthermore, we can't ever repay him and will always be indebted to him (see Mosiah 2:22–24). Don't you think Butch would have eventually figured out that hitting the fence was more painful than the cookie was good? Maybe you've discovered that the rewards of obedience sometimes don't seem worth the sacrifice.

I think the reason Butch persisted in trying to leap the fence had a lot to do with love. You might argue that dogs can't love, but what else can you call the affection between a dog and its master? If it wasn't fear or the hope of a reward that motivated him, then it must have had something to do with his feelings for me.

The scribes not only knew the script and wore the costumes, they loved the play. They did all the right things and went to great lengths to preserve the stories and traditions that illustrated the law. For all their commitment, however, the scribes somehow missed the performance. Like a stagehand who was worried about the props, the scribes admired the setting but somehow missed experiencing the emotion the play was supposed to evoke. Their love for the law prevented them from loving Christ. Like the scribes, we can get caught up in acting like Church members but miss the opportunity to be committed and fail to undergo the mighty change in our hearts the gospel is capable of causing (see Mosiah 5:2).

HYPOCRITES

Why do you obey the Lord's commandments? Christ said: "If ye love me, keep my commandments" (John 14:15). My feeling is that our love for Heavenly Father and for the Savior is the only power strong enough to keep us faithful. Any other motivation simply won't suffice when we are up against temptation and trials. In fact, the scriptures teach us: "He that saith, I know him, and keepeth not his commandments, is a liar [hypocrite?], and the truth is not in him. But whoso keepeth his word, in him verily is the love of God perfected" (1 John 2:4–5). We cannot truthfully say that we even know God if we don't keep his commandments.

Just as the scribes and Pharisees were guilty of doing the right thing for the wrong reason, we can be guilty of promoting the understanding of the law over obedience to the law. How do we become authentic instead of actors? Joseph Smith was confused by the hypocrisies of religion when he was a teenager (see JS—H 1:8). The answer Joseph received can help us identify the hypocrisies in our lives.

After being confronted by the power of darkness, seeing a pillar of light descending gradually, and being introduced to the Son of God, Joseph asked his question: which church should he join? Imagine his surprise when he was told to join none of them. At that very moment, Joseph also learned a profound lesson on hypocrisy. Christ explained that Joseph shouldn't join those churches for these five reasons:

1. They were all wrong.
2. Their creeds were abominable.
3. Their professors were all corrupt.

4. They drew near to God with their lips, but their hearts were far from him.
5. They taught for doctrines the commandments of men, which had a form of godliness but denied the power of God (JS–H 1:19).

Wouldn't it be ironic if members of the true Church of Jesus Christ were guilty of the very hypocrisies that tainted the churches in 1820? These five principles lend themselves to five serious personal questions relating to integrity (the opposite of hypocrisy). I invite you to take an integrity test:

1. Are you right (correct)?
2. Do you believe in anything that is abominable?
3. Are you corrupt (i.e., are your actions righteous)?
4. Do you follow Christ in both your words and your actions?
5. Do you know and follow God's (not man's) commandments?

Answering "no" or "sometimes" to any of the previous questions may indicate a need to put away hypocrisy and with full purpose of heart more closely follow the Lord. Only wholehearted attempts to follow him will ensure that we are not guilty of hypocrisy. Let's act our part and accept our roles in God's great play so we each may be found honest at the judgment day.

Kim M. Peterson is a seminary coordinator and institute instructor in the Denver, Colorado, area. He loves to ski and has been employed as a ski instructor during the winter months. Kim also enjoys cooking a variety of Eastern dishes. He and his wife, Terri, are the parents of a son and a daughter.

14

"WHAT LACK I YET?"

Clifford Rhoades

One of the happiest moments in my life was when I entered the waters of baptism and became a member of The Church of Jesus Christ of Latter-day Saints. When I came up out of the water, Elder Bybee gave me a big hug and whispered in my ear, "Welcome home, Cliff, welcome home." The feeling that entered into my heart when I heard those words spread like wildfire throughout my entire body. I felt as though I really had "come home!" The complete peace that I then experienced was in sharp contrast to the feelings of doubt and confusion I had gotten as I investigated other churches or religions in search of answers to some pretty tough questions about life and death and God. Through the things they taught me during my conversion process, Elder Bybee and Elder Otis helped me begin the continuing process that has led me to a strong personal testimony.

So what is a testimony, anyway? I like the way Elder Glenn L. Pace describes it. He says that a testimony refers "to having received a *spiritual witness* that (1) Jesus is the Christ; (2) Joseph Smith is a prophet of God and was the vehicle through whom the Lord restored the fulness of the gospel and delivered a second witness to Christ known as the Book of Mormon; (3) succeeding prophets received and continue to receive revelation from the Lord relative to our current challenges and the establishment of the kingdom of God on earth; and (4) each of us is entitled to personal revelation in the regulation of our own lives as we live the gospel"(*Spiritual Plateaus* [1991], 4; emphasis added).

A spiritual witness? I have had youth of the Church tell me that they have never had a spiritual witness of anything and really don't know if they even have a testimony. I can relate to that. I bet that you have had an experience similar to this somewhere as you were growing up.

I would go to sacrament meetings or firesides where others in attendance would say afterward that the Spirit was so thick in the meeting that you could cut it with a knife. I would smile and say something intelligent like, "Yeah! It was cool!" yet on the inside, I wouldn't feel a thing. Because I hadn't felt anything while everyone else around me had, I assumed I didn't have much of a testimony. After all, if the Spirit was so thick that you could cut it with a knife and I hadn't felt it, that must mean there was something wrong with me. Perhaps I just didn't have a testimony.

When I expressed that concern to the elders, Elder Bybee asked me to try an experiment. The first thing he did was to flip to a picture of the Savior in his missionary manual. Then he asked me to take the next minute or so to think about all the things that I knew about the Savior and my relationship with Him. After a couple of minutes had passed, Elder Bybee asked me to share one or two of my thoughts with him. As I did so, a peaceful, quiet spirit settled in the room and into my heart. It was similar to the feeling I had experienced when I was baptized.

As I finished relating my thoughts to Elder Bybee, he asked if I felt "it." I smiled at him and just nodded my head yes. He told me that the "it" that I was feeling was the Holy Ghost testifying to my spirit that the things that I had just said were true. Then he told me that one doesn't need to see Christ or angels or witness a miracle to gain a testimony. Rather, the Spirit most often comes quietly, unnoticed by others, and whispers peace to one's heart.

Elder Bybee then taught me a lesson that I think every missionary teaches. He taught me that the Spirit will tell you things are true in your heart long before your mind can pick them up. He urged me to trust my heart and the feelings of peace the Spirit brings.

I asked him about the fireside where the Spirit was supposed to have been so strong, but where I hadn't felt anything. Why hadn't I felt what others described? Instead of answering my question, he asked me what kind of feelings or experiences was I looking for—angels, voices, what? In a kindly way, he explained that rather than looking for spectacular manifestations, I should seek to experience that quiet, peaceful feeling he had helped me identify.

Ever since that day, whenever I go to a meeting, conference, the temple, or anywhere the Spirit is invited to be, I try to listen first with my heart. I listen for the feeling of peace. I challenge you youth of the noble birthright to try this little experiment with Christ or with the prophet or even the Church itself, that Elder Bybee conducted with me. And as you ponder and think about what things are right about each of these things, the Spirit will settle and testify to you in a way that you will know that these things are true. I feel certain you will discover that you do have feelings—a testimony, really—about the Savior, the restoration of the gospel, the Church. The feelings may be weak at this point, but you nonetheless have a testimony of the truth.

So, how does one gain the rock solid kind of testimony that will weather the spiritual storms that surely lie ahead? It is a fact that spiritual storms await us, perhaps they are even at our door. Elder Henry B. Eyring of the Quorum of the Twelve Apostles states: "As the forces around us increase in intensity, whatever spiritual strength was once sufficient will not be enough. And whatever growth in spiritual strength we once thought was possible, greater growth will be made available to us. Both the need for spiritual strength and the opportunity to acquire it will increase at rates which we underestimate at our peril" (*Ensign,* Oct. 1999, 9).

The thing that will bolster a fragile testimony or strengthen an established testimony is found in something the Savior said. When it was suggested that his doctrines and teachings were peculiar and perhaps of his own making, his reply was: *"If any man will do his will, he shall know of the doctrine, whether it be of God, or whether I speak of myself"* (John 7:17; emphasis added). And you thought Nike was the original creator of the idea behind the slogan "Just Do It!" It was the Lord who first said that if you want to know truth, then live the law of the gospel you wish to prove.

Elder John A. Widtsoe of the Quorum of the Twelve Apostles explained it this way: "I was brought up in scientific laboratories, where I was taught to test things, never to be satisfied unless a thing was tested. We have the right to test the Gospel of the Lord Jesus Christ. By testing it I mean living it, trying it out. Do you question the Word of Wisdom? Try it. Do you question the law of tithing? Practice it. Do you doubt the virtue of attending meetings? Attend them. Only then shall we be able to speak of these things intelligently and in such a way as to be respected by those who listen to us. Those who live the Gospel of Jesus Christ gain this higher knowledge, this greater testimony, this ultimate assurance that this is the truth" (in Conference Report, Oct. 1938, 129).

With the thought in mind of *doing it,* allow me to introduce you to a process of conversion that I call the Three-Month Experiment. To perform this experiment, you must be willing to follow the seven steps suggested for ninety straight days without missing.

STEP 1: HAVE AN INTENSE DESIRE FOR TRUTH, BE A TRUTH SEEKER, MEDITATE, AND DON'T GIVE UP

As in all attempts to gain something of worth, the desire to accomplish the goal has to outweigh the reluctance to do the hard work required to obtain the goal. When I was a young boy, I was diagnosed with diabetes and was told that I would have to take two to three shots of insulin a day to stay alive. Well, that was motivation enough to endure the shots, even though I was deathly afraid of needles at that time in my life.

Trying to keep the amount of sugar in my blood under control kept me on a health roller coaster. I think I stayed four-foot-nothing and sixty- five pounds for several years. That I was so scrawny was somewhat embarrassing to me since both my older brothers were big and strong and quite athletic. Me, I was a klutz. But by the time I was in eighth grade, I had developed an intense desire to be an athlete.

My dad bought me some weights, and I started lifting and running, sometimes to the extent that I would make myself sick. I remember some hot summer days when I would spend hours bucking bales of hay onto a wagon and then go home to do my workout routine, wondering if all that effort was worth it. Progress seemed so slow and there wasn't any immediate dynamic increase in my athletic ability.

I was once told that the character of an individual is a reflection of that person's ability to follow a decision through after the emotion that led to the decision is spent. If that's true, there were many days where my character was truly tested. But I stayed with it, and by the time I graduated from high school I had earned an athletic scholarship to play football and was named Athlete of the Year at my high school. I had met my goal and fulfilled a childhood desire.

Gaining the kind of testimony the missionaries had seemed to me to require as much work, if not more, than trying to control my diabetes and become athletic. Elder Bybee told me once that just as obedience to the physical laws of God resulted in the achievement of physical goals or athletic abilities, applying spiritual laws would also help me to achieve spiritual goals! I would just have to show the Lord that I had a wholehearted desire and continue to exercise faith, even if I couldn't immediately tell if anything was really happening. So, the first step to solidifying a testimony is to sincerely *desire* to succeed despite obstacles or opposition.

STEP 2: CLEAN THE SLATE OF YOUR LIFE BEFORE YOU EVEN START SEEKING A TESTIMONY

President Spencer W. Kimball assures us that "the Lord has promised repeatedly that he will give you a knowledge of spiritual things when you have placed yourself in a proper frame of mind" (*The Teachings of Spencer W. Kimball,* [1982], 63). That proper frame of mind is one where you know that you are clean from the errors of this life and are making the effort to do right. This cleansing process might involve changing harmful habits. Stop drinking beverages that are physically harmful to you. This will certainly include alcohol and perhaps drinks containing caffeine. Stop smoking, chewing tobacco, or using drugs. One cannot confidently invite the Spirit into one's life while in violation of the Word of Wisdom. Keep yourself morally clean and in harmony with the principles of virtue taught by the Savior.

If you sincerely desire to have a spiritual experience, you may also wish to sacrifice some personal pleasures that are not in and of themselves sinful—demonstrating to the Lord in this way the strength of your desire. You might consider giving up listening to music or viewing materials that are incompatible with the Spirit of the Lord. I know some young people who, in their quest to gain a testimony, have given up watching television or videos or going to movies entirely for the three months. It will also help to keep a journal, focusing in your daily entries on the commitments you are making and describing the spiritual feelings that come to you.

STEP 3: ATTEND ALL YOUR CHURCH MEETINGS AND LISTEN CAREFULLY TO WHAT IS BEING SAID

Take your journal with you wherever you go and record

insights that come to you as a result of the things you hear or experience. You don't have to write the words you are hearing word for word, but rather record the feelings you experience as you listen to the speakers present their messages. Write down those things the Spirit impresses you to write.

STEP 4: PRAY MORNING AND NIGHT

Make these prayers of thanksgiving and gratitude. As you go through the day, notice how many times you talk to yourself and then consciously treat these conversations as if you were talking to the Lord. Think of him standing next to you as you speak to him. As you do this, you will begin to understand how it is possible to constantly carry a prayer in your heart. This conversing with the Lord with every thought that you are thinking will become an attitude of meditation that will allow the Spirit to work with you and teach you.

STEP 5: SERVE SOMEONE AROUND YOU EVERY DAY BY PERFORMING RANDOM ACTS OF KINDNESS

There is something wonderfully fulfilling about doing something nice for someone else, particularly when the act is spontaneous and unexpected. It doesn't have to be something big, fancy, or showy. In fact, it is often more fun to do these kinds of things anonymously. To begin, aim your first random acts of kindness at the members of your family. Can you imagine the effect it might have on your parents or a brother or a sister when you perform some small, unexpected service for them? Then you might look outside of the family circle, to someone you perhaps don't get along with all that well, or to strangers. I promise you that doing nice things for others will provide a feeling of satisfaction and invite the Spirit into your life. As you do these acts of kindness, also look for opportunities to share your testimony with those you are serving. Take advantage of fast and testimony day in your ward by bearing a short testimony of things you hope to learn in this experiment, or of the feelings you have had from doing these acts of kindness.

STEP 6: FIND SOMETHING DAILY AROUND YOU IN NATURE THAT TESTIFIES OF A GOSPEL DOCTRINE

"And behold, all things have their likeness, and all things are created and made to bear record of me, both things which are temporal, and things which are spiritual; things which are in the heavens above, and things which are on the earth, and things which are in the earth, and things which are under the earth, both above and beneath: all things bear record of me" (Moses 6:63).

This scripture teaches us that ALL things bear testimony and are a witness to Christ and our Heavenly Father. What this part of the experiment will eventually teach us is how to look at the world with greater gratitude and through spiritual eyes.

STEP 7: CREATE YOUR OWN SCHEDULE OF READING THE SCRIPTURES

During this three-month period, plan to read the five Gospels (Matthew, Mark, Luke, John, and 3 Nephi) and then the rest of the Book of Mormon from cover to cover. Offer a prayer each time you read, asking for understanding and the spirit of revelation and of prophesy, that you might know the Lord, the reality of the Restoration, and the truthfulness of the Church.

Following these seven steps will invite the Spirit of the Lord into your life. But keep in mind that spiritual manifestations cannot be forced. Spiritual experiences come as gifts to those who have shown a desire and demonstrated an effort to follow the Savior.

When I first tried this experiment, I didn't get the results that I desired. I think in my first attempt I was looking for some kind of miraculous witness. Then in an early morning institute class, I learned an interesting doctrine about testimonies. Our instructor was making the point that testimonies that are gained by miracles do not always hold up in the face of everyday trials. As evidence of this, he cited the story of Christ feeding the five thousand and the negative response of the people the next day when Christ refused to feed them again. Brother Perrett pointed out to us that their faith was shallow and rested on what the Savior could do for them. When the Lord didn't measure up to their expectations by doing what they wanted him to do, they turned away and followed him no more (see John 6:66).

Brother Perrett then directed our attention to the place where Jesus asked his disciples, "Whom do men say that I the Son of man am?" (Matthew 16:13). Responding for himself and the others, Peter answered: "Thou art the Christ, the Son of the living God" (v. 16). Jesus then made a statement that deeply impressed me. He said that "flesh and blood hath not revealed it unto thee, but my Father which is in heaven" (v. 17). Reading that, I realized for the first time that a testimony is built upon the rock of revelation, which comes to every individual and must be renewed daily, if that testimony is to continue growing.

From that moment on, I tried doing everything that would allow revelation to build my testimony. I followed the three-month experiment with renewed determination. I prayed, I read my scriptures, I fasted, and I paid tithing. I felt that I was doing all right until I came in contact with some old friends who asked me some questions about the Church and about Joseph Smith, which I had no idea how to answer. The thing that bothered me the most wasn't that I didn't know how to answer their questions but that my testimony had little to no effect in their lives. As I later shared my frustration with some good friends, I was shown this scripture:

"And, behold, one came and said unto him, Good Master, what good thing shall I do, that I may have eternal life?

"And he said unto him, Why callest thou me good? there is none good but one, that is, God: but if thou wilt enter into life, keep the commandments.

"He saith unto him, Which? Jesus said, Thou shalt do no murder, Thou shalt not commit adultery, Thou shalt not steal, Thou shalt not bear false witness,

"Honour thy father and thy mother: and, Thou shalt love thy neighbour as thyself.

"The young man saith unto him, All these things have I kept from my youth up: ***what lack I yet?***

"Jesus said unto him, If thou wilt be perfect, go and sell that thou hast, and give to the poor, and thou shalt have treasure in heaven: and come and follow me.

"But when the young man heard that saying, he went away sorrowful: for he had great possessions" (Matthew 19:16–22; emphasis added).

One of my friends, Nancy, then said to me that I had been doing all the technical things necessary to gain and keep a testimony but that I was perhaps missing the heart of what a testimony is really all about. I needed to have the courage to surrender entirely to Christ.

At that time, my love of running was one of the most important things in my life. And I was doing some major training in the hope I might qualify for the mile in the U. S. Olympic trials. Now, for just a moment, ask yourself, what is your greatest treasure—what do you value most in life? Like I said, at that time my legs were my most treasured possession. Suppose Christ were to come to you and ask you to give him the thing you value most.

My friends asked me that question. I have to admit, I thought about being in a wheelchair, and that didn't excite me very much. My grandfather was in a wheelchair, and it didn't look like much fun. After pondering the question, I said something to the effect, "I guess if Christ really wants my legs, he can have them."

My friends responded, "If you are not willing to give

Christ that which he asks for, you love whatever it is too much."

That idea really bothered me. I was willing to live the life the Three-Month Experiment demanded, but was I willing to give my all to Christ once I learned of him? Was I asking for a million-dollar answer from the Lord but giving only a ten-dollar effort? I began the experiment again, but this time I approached the Lord and asked what I lacked to receive an answer. The answer came in the form of a question—a question we might all do well to ask ourselves: "When you receive the testimony you say you want, what will you do with it?"

That hit me hard because I already knew in my heart what the Lord expected, and it was not what I had planned on doing. My plan, as stated earlier, was to train to become an Olympic athlete. The Lord's plan was for me to serve a full-time mission, even at the age of twenty-two. When I finally agreed to the Lord's plan, if I could gain a stronger testimony, I began the experiment over again. I had a wonderful experience during those three months, doing the seven-step experiment and gaining in the process a stronger testimony.

But as I look back at that time in my life, I am able to see that the real strengthening of my testimony, the strengthening that will allow me to endure the spiritual storms that lie ahead, that strengthening came when I entered the mission field and served the Lord for two full years.

While on my mission, I had an experience that exposed me to a method our Father in Heaven uses to help us learn about how strong our testimonies really are. I call it the doctrine of "walking alone, at times, to learn of God." There are several scriptural accounts that suggest the Father periodically leaves us to ourselves to test our ability to walk as God would have us walk.

Moses had such an experience. After having had a marvelous spiritual manifestation, in which he was shown the expanse of God's creation and the whole of the human race, "The presence of God withdrew from Moses, . . . and Moses was left unto himself" (Moses 1:9). Deprived of the Spirit of the Lord, Moses is then tempted by Satan, who invites Moses to worship him. But calling upon God, Moses receives strength and is able to dispatch Satan (see vv. 12–22). Immediately, the Lord comes back and blesses Moses for remaining true to the knowledge that was given to him in the prior spiritual experience.

We can trace this pattern in the life of Joseph Smith as well. Joseph receives a divine manifestation, the greatest theophany of modern time, and then is left virtually "unto himself" for the next three years. Perhaps in such times of trial and tribulation we are expected to prove ourselves true even without the benefit of the influence of the Spirit. Our challenge is to be righteous at all times, under all conditions and circumstances.

I came to realize that I will have times in my life where I may feel my testimony isn't growing. But in reality, it may be during these times of being alone that I will grow the most. I believe it is at these times that I am showing my Father in Heaven that my testimony is strong enough to carry me through whatever the situation may be. And then as I endure it well, when I come back into the warmth of his spirit, my testimony will have grown even more than I could have expected and in ways that I could not have imagined.

In conclusion, I would like to leave with you a saying that was given to me on a plaque by Elder Bybee. It is a good saying to have memorized and to remember often. It has helped me countless times in keeping my value system right and my desires in line with what I feel the Father expects of me.

It is good to be a seeker,
But soon, one must be a finder.
And then it is well, to give what

One has found, a gift unto the world,
For whoever will accept it.
Anonymous

May the gift you give to the world and to your friends and family be a testimony that has been forged in the furnace of spiritual experiences and written deep within your heart. I had searched for this Church all my life and am eternally grateful to a young woman who shared her strong testimony with me when I was looking for a God who loved me. I am extremely grateful to the Lord for allowing me the opportunity to be able to serve a full-time mission and learn firsthand of God's love for his children and the powers associated with the priesthood.

I bear you my testimony that The Church of Jesus Christ of Latter-day Saints is Christ's true Church, that Christ did all that the scriptures testify that he did, and that he personally knows and loves you. I testify that there are no secrets he does not know or broken dreams that he does not understand or shattered lives his hands cannot touch and heal. May the Lord bless your efforts to gain your own testimony, and may your testimony shine as a lighthouse to those, like I was, who are struggling in darkness to find true light but do not know where to look.

Clifford Rhoades has been a seminary instructor for nineteen years and has worked with the BYU Department of Religion for three years. He has also worked in Texas as the institute of religion coordinator for UTA, TCU, and SMU. He currently resides in Idaho Falls, Idaho, where he teaches seminary. He was a convert to the Church at age twenty-two and later served a mission in Ventura, California. Cliff and his wife were married in the Idaho Falls Temple and have four daughters. He has been a survival teacher and loves all outdoor activities. A former bishop, he currently serves as a stake Young Men president.

15

"WHAT E'ER THOU ART, ACT WELL THY PART!"

Matthew O. Richardson

I can still picture a frustrated, angry sixth-grader standing defiantly atop his desk and shouting at our teacher: "I don't need you!" His face was flushed, and he panted as he fought to control his emotions and keep from crying. His attempts, however, were in vain. As tears began to roll down his cheeks, Pat looked around the room and softly added: "I don't need any of you." He then clenched his teeth and resolutely yelled: "I don't need *anyone!*"

The room fell silent. I didn't want to look up at Pat, and I didn't dare look at our teacher, Mr. Worlund. Like most of my classmates, I feared that Pat had crossed a line that would bring about death or, at a minimum, dismemberment. After all, Mr. Worlund was an ex-marine, who had told us on the first day of school that he could "kill a man with his thumb!" Could Pat have forgotten that? Surely he was a dead man.

"That's not true, Pat," Mr. Worlund said calmly as he stood up from his desk. I remember keeping my head down but raising my eyes to watch as Mr. Worlund walked slowly toward Pat and stopped in front of him. "You do need other people."

"No, I don't!" Pat responded. I was shocked that Pat didn't back down and surprised at how calmly Mr. Worlund was responding to the challenge.

"Yes, Pat, you do," Mr. Worlund said. "What are you going to eat for dinner?" I wasn't quite sure what dinner had to do with the present situation, but Pat barked back: "I can make my own sandwiches."

"Ah," Mr. Worlund said, nodding his head as if he knew something we didn't know. "So you'll use your parents' bread, then?"

"No," Pat shot back, "I'll buy my own bread. . . . I don't need anybody!"

Mr. Worlund kept his hands (and deadly thumbs) in his pockets and continued calmly by saying: "But who will make the bread you're going to eat or bake that bread or grow the wheat?" Pat didn't know what to say.

"Who is going to give you a job so you can buy your own bread, or who will print the money? Who is going to make your clothes, sell your clothes, or provide the electricity you use?"

Mr. Worlund was on a roll. "Pat, you *do* need others, we *all* need others." He paused just long enough, like he usually did whenever he wanted to emphasize something, and then said: "And *we* need you, Pat."

I haven't forgotten that experience even though it happened many years ago, and I have often thought about what might drive a sixth-grader to stand defiantly on a desk and put his life under the lethal thumb of an ex-marine.

But haven't we all felt a little like Pat at one time or another? There are in every life those frustrating moments of self-doubt, despair, discouragement, or failure when, imagining a bleak personal future, we might be pushed to the edge—when we might convince ourselves that we don't need anyone else and that they don't need us. Such is the case especially when those we care most about have offended us, disappointed us, or maybe even abandoned us. It is those feelings of isolation and loneliness that I want to discuss.

Let's begin by talking about personal ecology. I know that when I use the word *ecology,* most of you will think immediately of biology, recycling, polluted ponds, and things like that. And you'd be right to do so because ecology is a science that deals with the relationships between living things and their environment and with each other. But that doesn't happen only in nature. Ecology is a fact of life in human relationships, too. Simply put, what you do affects not only your surroundings but others as well—even when you might think otherwise.

Think of it this way. Just as one person, dumping toxic waste into a stream, creates a ripple effect that impacts the environment, animals, and humans (both those now living and future generations), so do your attitudes, actions, and decisions have an effect on your family, friends, and community. Each of us is an inseparable part of the whole picture.

With this concept of personal ecology in mind, think of President David O. McKay and a life-altering experience he had while serving as a young missionary in Scotland. Arriving in a foreign country and discovering the work to be discouraging, Elder McKay found himself homesick and disheartened. One day he and his companion spent some time sight-seeing, walking around Stirling Castle, feeling sorry for themselves and neglecting their missionary duties. As they walked back through town, they passed a building that was under construction. Inscribed on a stone arch over one of the doorways was this saying: "What e'er thou art, act well thy part." Immediately David O. McKay realized he was part of a greater work and needed to "act well" his missionary part (*Cherished Experiences* [1955], 174–75).

I have seen the very stone President McKay described. There are nine symbols carved into the stone. At a casual glance, the symbols appear to be nothing more than an abstract decoration. But the symbols are related to the inscription, and they teach a powerful lesson.

Each symbol represents a number, i.e., *five* fingers, the Roman numeral for *ten,* a *three*-sided triangle, etc. The interesting thing is that the sum of the numbers for every row and column is eighteen. This is also true when adding diagonally. Thus, each number is a vital part of the whole mathematical puzzle. If one number were changed, even just slightly, the magic would be gone, and the ecology (the relationship between the parts and the whole) would be lost. The mathematical significance of each number, when considered together, illustrates the phrase "What e'er thou art"—whether a five, a ten, or a three—"act well thy part."

The most important ecological system in life is the family. In "The Family: A Proclamation to the World," which was published by the First Presidency and the Council of the Twelve Apostles in 1995, our Church leaders declared: "The family is central to the Creator's plan for the eternal destiny of His children."

Some may be thinking, *If the family is so important to God, then why was I born into one as unhappy as mine?* I don't believe that God ever intended families to be unhappy. In fact, it isn't God, or the Church, that creates unhappy families. The condition of a family is the result (sum of) the actions of each individual member. It's a matter of how well each acts their part.

Those, such as Pat, who feel that they aren't needed or don't need others, especially in families, don't understand the ecology of family life. In a family, for things to add up, each member must act well his or her part.

BELONGING TO A FAMILY

Every person who reads this chapter belongs to some type of family. As you consider your connection with your family, please know that all families are different. Understanding the type of family you belong to also helps you determine how you should act your part. I realize there are some who feel that they don't have a family at all. Perhaps death, abandonment, divorce, neglect, or even abuse has separated you from your natural family ties. But everyone has the opportunity of belonging to a family.

I once gave a talk in a ward of college students about the enrichment, power, and protection available through a father's blessing. For as far back as I can remember, I received a priesthood blessing from my dad before the beginning of every school year. It always provided tremendous help and a sense of protection in my life, and giving my children a father's blessing at the beginning of each school year is now one of the treasured traditions in my own family.

In the week following my talk on this subject, several members of the congregation visited me. Each of these young people wanted to experience a father's blessing, but, for one reason or another, they didn't have the opportunity. Some were the only members of the Church in their family, others had lost their fathers to death, divorce, or inactivity. Although their circumstances differed, all of them had a sense of loss, disappointment, and pain, along with an inescapable feeling that they had some how been cheated.

When one understands the divine concept of family, however, no one need ever be deprived of belonging to and benefiting from a family. You see, in addition to our natural family ties, each of us is part of an extended family—a Church family, which ultimately fits into the divine family. I explained to each of these "fatherless" ward members that in spite of their circumstances, they still had access to a father's blessing. If their father was unable to bless them, for example, perhaps someone in their extended family could—a grandfather, uncle, or in-law. If no extended family member were available, they could turn to our ward family. This extended pattern provides that everyone's needs are met and that a family connection is always available.

YOUR PART IN THE FAMILY

There are those who feel the parents are the ones who determine the quality of a family. That is only partly true. Parents, like you, must "act well" their parts. So remember that each part of the magic square is dependent upon the other. Every member of the family contributes to the quality of family life. I have talked with some youth who feel that since their parents are not fulfilling their parental roles, he or she (the child) has no obligation to their family. The truth is that when other members of a family are not acting well their part, it may adversely affect the family, but it does not release anyone else from their role within the family. It doesn't really matter whether your parents are skillful or not, whether your siblings are spiteful or loving—you will always be a son or a daughter, a brother or a sister. You cannot escape your part in the bigger picture. So, then, what can a son or daughter do to act well their part?

1. Pray with and for your family. As a son or daughter, you should pray for your family. Too often we concentrate on the failings of our parents or siblings and complain that we are trapped. Though that may be so, we can pray for family members to overcome their weaknesses. "If children pray for their parents," President N. Eldon Tanner taught, "it makes them more appreciative of their parents, and as they pray for one another, they feel closer to one another." He continued by saying that when we pray for each other in families "we forget our differences and think of the best in others, and pray for their well-being and for strength to overcome our own weaknesses" (in Conference Report, Oct. 1967, 55–56). I hope that you will pray to your Heavenly Father in behalf of your earthy parents and siblings, as well as the members of your Church family.

2. Participate in family activities. Sometimes families are filled with contention because sons and daughters refuse to take an active part in the family. When we understand our role in any type of family, it becomes clear that the success of the family, ward, or Church greatly depends upon our willing participation. Your participation and cooperation in your family is vital if the family is to reach its potential. Can you think of a time when Laman or Lemuel wanted to do *anything* with their family? Since they couldn't see beyond their own needs and desires, they spent their lives complaining, being angry, and feeling robbed. They probably thought they were the only ones required to sacrifice. In reality, Laman and Lemuel were ecological family thugs. Their stubbornness not only affected themselves, but it affected everyone else in the family, including future generations. Their wrong-headed, selfish, and unrighteous behavior made them weak links in the family chain, and Lehi's family was eventually divided—emotionally, spiritually, and, finally, physically.

Modern-day murmuring and complaining diminish far too many family experiences. I am grateful to my older children, who willingly play hide-and-seek, not so much because they like the game, but because they like their three-year-old brother, who likes to hide. Any family activity requires the sacrifice of at least one member of the family. Not every family member likes to bowl, play or watch sports, or listen to classical, country, or rock music. We should participate in family activities, not because we like the activities, but because we love the family. Family members who either boycott the family activity altogether or who murmur before, during, and after family events, put a damper on things and create tension. This is a sure sign of selfishness.

Too many family prayers are marred by groans of resistance, and it is hard to hold a pleasant family home evening when someone asks, "How long is this going to last?" every few minutes. I have talked with thousands of youth and find it unfortunate that most of their families ceased holding family night, saying family prayers, reading the scriptures together, playing games together, or going on family vacations as soon as they or some of their siblings became teenagers. Nothing is more discouraging to parents than kids who roll their eyes, complain that everything is "boring," or otherwise let it be known they are too cool to any longer participate in family activities.

3. Maintain the higher law—strive always to lift other members of the family. If the members of the family participate in mediocre ways, mediocrity will prevail. When a member of a family is capable of making a bigger and better contribution, it is their obligation to be true to the higher way. Some of you may be the only member (or active member) of the Church in your family. If you feel and know certain things are true, you must act well your part. Never diminish your power by diluting or abandoning your belief. Keep the commandments to the best of your ability. Continue to say your prayers, encourage others in righteousness, and most importantly, set a proper and inspiring example.

4. Be a peacemaker. Paul outlined a simple formula for the successful operation of families. He wrote: "Husbands, love your wives, even as Christ also loved the church, and gave himself for it" (Ephesians 5:25). A sure sign that we love "even as Christ also loved" is when we (husbands, wives, sons, daughters, brothers, and sisters) give freely of ourselves to one another. Unlike Laman and Lemuel, Nephi, Sam, Jacob, and those who followed Christ, consistently gave of themselves. President Gordon B. Hinckley has taught that the root cause of broken homes is selfishness (see *Ensign,* May 1991, 71–74).

In the Sermon on the Mount, Christ taught: "Blessed are the peacemakers: for they shall be called the children of God" (Matthew 5:9). Peacemaking is an unselfish endeavor. The fruit of the peacemaker's work is peace and sanctuary. "If ever there was a time when we needed peacemakers," Elder Franklin D. Richards taught, "it is today" (*Ensign,* Nov. 1983, 57). Too many families, even great families, lack a spirit of peace and have instead the spirit of contention in their homes. Contention can be seen in our motives (why we do what we do), how we talk to each other, and how we treat each other. Contention is something that can be felt in a home, contributing to a feeling of tension, anger, and hostility. Contention drives out love. And contention is a manifestation of selfishness that, if unchecked, will devour the good of a family—just like cancer will devour a body.

Elder Franklin D. Richards told of a bishop who desired that every home in his ward would be a "bit of heaven on earth." He met with several young people in the ward and asked them to participate in an "experiment." He then challenged them to be peacemakers in their home for one month. "Whenever you are irritated . . . control yourself and help the others to control themselves," the bishop instructed. Part of the arrangement was not to tell anyone about his or her new mission and to report back to the bishop at the end of the month.

At the end of the month, one young man reported: "I had no idea I would have so much influence in my home. It's really been different this last month. I've been wondering if much of the turmoil and strife we used to have was caused by me and my attitudes." Others reported changes in feelings between siblings, a better overall spirit in the home, and a decrease in contention. In addition, I think this comment, from a young woman who participated in the experiment, is not only interesting but also vitally important. She said: "Yes, there has been a much sweeter and cooperative and unselfish spirit in our home since I began this experiment, but the biggest difference of all has been in me. I've tried hard to be a good example and a peacemaker, and I feel better about myself than I have ever felt. A wonderful feeling of peace has come over me" (*Ensign,* Nov. 1983, 57–58). When we act well in our part, we, as individuals, benefit as much as others. I challenge you to perform the same experiment in your family.

Nothing gives me greater pleasure, as a parent, than watching my children talk, laugh, pray, and play together. Nothing pains me more than to watch them hurtfully tease or be rude or mean to each other. We can practice peacemaking in our homes by resisting the temptation to be critical or to judge others and by practicing forgiveness, forgetting the past, and being more patient and flexible.

Whenever tension begins to arise in our home, I say: "Give me a quack!" After some coaxing, my children will "quack" like a duck, and it usually makes us laugh and lightens the moment. This family joke originated at a time when something was causing contention in our family because someone was taking something far too seriously. As you know, water slides right off a duck's back so that before it can cause a problem, it is gone. I suggested that if we would just refrain from making selfish demands, teasing each other, being sarcastic, and doing little everyday things that bug one another, and if they would let hard feelings roll off—like water off a duck's back—we would all be happier and better off. On a whim, I asked the two children who were at odds to be more like ducks and "give me a quack." They did so, and we had a new family tradition. This silly practice usually lightens the mood, decreases the tension, and puts things back into perspective. After all, it's awfully hard to be angry when you are quacking like a duck!

5. To understand family roles and get advice on dealing with problems, turn to the scriptures. A great resource in dealing with problems in a family is the scriptures. There you can read about people who had struggles with parents, siblings, and other relatives. You can also read about families who seemed to have things going in the right direction. If you have an unrighteous family member, for example, you'll want to read about how Nephi dealt with his disobedient brothers. If you have offended someone in your family, read about Jacob and Esau and how they resolved their differences. The scriptures provide endless examples of family interaction and serve as an inspired resource for modern application.

6. Be hopeful. Regardless of your family situation, you can always turn to two family members who will never abandon you: God, our Heavenly Father, and Jesus Christ, our spiritual Brother. They are wonderful models of those who act well their part when it comes to family roles. Additionally, they have promised peace and comfort to those who join the ranks of their family. As part of that heavenly family, you are promised that if you "continue in the faith grounded and settled, and be not moved away from the hope of the gospel," you and your family, will be "reconciled" and have all the fulness of the Father (see Colossians 1:19–23).

CONCLUSION

Whatever your part (son/daughter, sibling, Church brother/sister, or son/daughter of God), it is your responsibility to act well. President Gordon B. Hinckley has admonished us to "never become a weak link in the chain of your family's generations. Do whatever you are asked to do and do it with a glad heart" (*Church News,* 4 Dec. 1999, 7). None of us can afford to be the weak link. You may be the only member of the Church or perhaps the only *active* member in your family. If so, you have an added responsibility and much is expected of you. You may have to say your prayers in your closet, exercise patience, and endure terrible circumstances—nevertheless, stay strong and forge ahead with conviction and faith. Why? For the sake of the chain that links together you, a future spouse and children, and all of us who are members of the Church. You need us, and we need you.

My father is a convert to the Church. He was baptized when I was a very young child. Later in life, I realized that when he joined the Church, he was ostracized by his family. As a result, he wasn't very welcome in his family circle. I can only imagine his pain. They were often cruel to him, to my mother, and to my siblings and me. When I was younger, I wondered why we would drive across the country to family reunions where we weren't welcome, pray for my indifferent aunts, uncles, and cousins, and send them presents and cards on holidays. If anyone had an excuse to be angry or spiteful or to even quit trying to act well his part as a son and brother, it was my father. I couldn't understand why he would keep trying, always acting nobly, and hoping for some type of change.

I now know the answer. My father is a good man. He is a good father. But the reason he is a good man and a good father is because he tried to be a good son, brother, member of the Church, and son of God. Even when he wasn't wanted, he tried to act well his part.

Someday you will probably have a family of your own. You will assume a new role—husband, wife, father, or mother. More than likely you will act out your new part in a similar way, with the same intensity and effort, you are now acting out your part as a son, daughter, brother, or sister. I am grateful that my parents have been strong links in my family chain. I can't imagine what might have happened had they decided they didn't need anybody else and that no one needed them. You see, my life—my chain—is directly linked to them. My wife and my children are directly linked to me. We (you and I) are likewise linked together in a Church family and a divine family. The strength of our lives depends upon the strength of the family. The strength of the family depends upon the strength of its parts. May each of us always treasure our connection with the families to which we belong and always remember: "What e'er thou art, act well thy part."

Matthew O. Richardson is an assistant professor at Brigham Young University in the Department of Church History and Doctrine. He served a mission to Denmark and holds a doctoral degree in Educational Leadership. Matt enjoys sports, traveling, and making Mickey Mouse pancakes on Saturday mornings. He is passionate about his family and the gospel. He and his wife, Lisa, have four children.

16

FEASTING UPON THE WORD

R. Scott Simmons

"And that from a child thou hast known the holy scriptures, which are able to make thee wise unto salvation through faith which is in Christ Jesus.

"All scripture is given by inspiration of God, and is profitable for doctrine, for reproof, for correction, for instruction in righteousness" (2 Timothy 3:15–16).

I love the scriptures. I have reached a point in my life where it is difficult for me to let a day go by without reading my scriptures. For me, if I miss a day of reading, it's like going without food—spiritually speaking. The hunger that I experience is real and needs to be satisfied. I have found that the only way to completely satisfy this hunger is to "feast upon the words of Christ" (2 Nephi 32:3).

I feel this way now, but it wasn't always the case. There was a time when I really struggled to read the scriptures. As a result I was starving spiritually, and I didn't realize it.

My struggle came when I was about your age. I had been taught that the scriptures were important, and so I tried to read them. However, I found the language hard to understand—all the thees, thous, and thines, not to mention all the different names and places I couldn't pronounce. Also, there were many places where I just didn't get what was going on. I was often frustrated and would just stop reading. Then, I would attend a lesson or hear a talk on the importance of the scriptures and try reading again, only to end up frustrated once more.

All the while, I was really struggling personally. I didn't realize it at the time, but my struggles were a result of spiritual malnutrition. I was hungry for something but didn't know what it was. Does any of this sound familiar, even a little? If it does, maybe I can help. As I said, things are completely different now. The language is still tough to decipher sometimes, and there are even times when I am still not sure what is going on, but I don't get frustrated. I even enjoy those difficult scriptures, even though I admit I don't completely understand them. So what made the difference? Let me show you.

First, I know you already know the scriptures are important, but do you know just *how* important? Here is what President Ezra Taft Benson had to say: "Success in righteousness, the power to avoid deception and resist temptation, guidance in our daily lives, healing of the soul—these are but a few of the promises the Lord has given to those who will come to His word. Does the Lord promise and not fulfill? Surely if He tells us that these things will come to us if we lay hold upon His word, then the blessings can be ours. And if we do not, then the blessings may be lost. *However diligent we may be in other areas, certain blessings are to be found only in the scriptures, only in coming to the word of the Lord and holding fast to it as we make our way through the mists of darkness to the tree of life"* (*Ensign*, May 1986, 82; emphasis added).

Did you catch what President Benson said at the end of this quote? "Certain blessings are to be found only in the scriptures." That is important to note. You can be doing everything else right, but if you are not reading your scriptures, you are missing out on some important blessings. Just what are those blessings? President Benson gives a clue at the end of his quote. Did you notice he mentioned the tree of life? What does that have to do with scripture reading?

Remember Father Lehi's vision? In it, he saw "a tree, whose fruit was desirable to make one happy. . . . And as [he] partook of the fruit thereof it filled [his] soul with exceedingly great joy" (1 Nephi 8:10, 12).

A tree bearing fruit that will make you happy and fill your soul with joy? Sounds good, doesn't it? Later on, Nephi tells us what this tree and fruit represent. He says, "It is the love of God, which sheddeth itself abroad in the hearts of the children of men; wherefore, it is the most desirable above all things" (1 Nephi 11:22).

The fruit that Lehi ate, which made him happy and filled him with joy, was the love of God. According to Lehi and Nephi there is nothing better than to experience God's love. I agree. Yes, I have also eaten this fruit. I have felt God's love for me, and I testify that Lehi's description is true. To feel the love of God makes you happy and fills your soul with joy.

That is pretty incredible, isn't it? But, wait. There is something else to consider. Lehi saw other people trying to make their way to the tree, but something got in their way. Remember the mist of darkness? Nephi tells us that "the mists of darkness are the temptations of the devil, which blindeth the eyes, and hardeneth the hearts of the children of men, and leadeth them away into broad roads, that they perish and are lost" (1 Nephi 12:17). The adversary is doing everything he can to keep us from eating that fruit. The last thing he wants for us is happiness and joy. Instead, "he seeketh that all men might be *miserable* like unto himself" (2 Nephi 2:27; emphasis added). These mists of darkness are thick today. Again, listen to what President Benson has said about them:

"The Apostle Paul saw our day. He described it as a time

when such things as blasphemy, dishonesty, cruelty, unnatural affection, pride and pleasure seeking would abound (see 2 Timothy 3:17). He also warned that 'evil men and seducers would wax worse and worse, deceiving and being deceived' (2 Timothy 3:12). Such grim predictions by prophets of old would be cause for great fear and discouragement if those same prophets had not, at the same time, offered the solution. In their inspired counsel we can find the answer to the spiritual crises of our age" (*The Teachings of Ezra Taft Benson* [1988], 88).

What is that inspired counsel? What can help us make it through the mists of darkness, so we can arrive safely at the tree and partake of the fruit? Or, in other words, what will help us see through Satan's temptations and make the choices that will help us feel God's love, which makes us happy and brings us joy? The answer is again found in Lehi's dream. He saw something else—something that helped the people find their way through the mist of darkness. It was a "rod of iron, and it extended along the bank of the river, and led to the tree" (1 Nephi 8:19).

Nephi later told his brothers that the rod of iron is "the word of God; and [that] whoso would hearken unto the word of God, and would hold fast unto it, they would never perish; neither could the temptations and the fiery darts of the adversary overpower them unto blindness, to lead them away to destruction" (1 Nephi 15:24).

So, the rod of iron is the word of God—the scriptures. Isn't that incredible? The scriptures can lead you through the mist of darkness and right to the tree. We just need to hold fast to the rod. What does that mean? Simply put, we need to read every day.

Well, now you know that if you read your scriptures daily, they will help you overcome the temptations of Satan and feel God's love. But, what if that's not happening? What if the scriptures aren't doing that for you? What if you just get frustrated the way I used to? Well, first of all, knowing that the result of reading the scriptures is the love of God, which brings us happiness and joy should help. You now know, if you didn't before, that reading the scriptures is well worth the effort it takes. However, there are some other principles that may help.

First, I believe that it takes effort to achieve good things. Our Father in Heaven expects us to do our part. Think about the example of Oliver Cowdery in his unsuccessful attempts to translate the plates. Explaining why Oliver had failed, the Lord told him, "Behold, you have not understood; you have supposed that I would give it unto you, when you took no thought save it was to ask me" (D&C 9:7). Oliver hadn't done his part. What can we do to do our part?

Well, it sounds simple, but one thing you have to do is read—every day. I have found that it helps me if I set aside a regular time to read my scriptures. For me the best time is first thing in the morning before I get busy with all the things that fill my day. But you don't have to read in the morning. You could read during lunch or after school or before dinner or in the evening. Just a word of caution here: most of my students who try to read right before they go to bed, often find they are so tired that they are only able to read for a couple of minutes. I learned a great lesson about this kind of scripture study while visiting a ward in Canada.

I had flown up to speak and was there over a Sunday. So, I found a local ward I could attend. Being unfamiliar with the area, I got a little lost and arrived late. I found a place in the back of the chapel and took a seat.

The meeting was wonderful. It was a missionary farewell. As usual the family of the departing missionary spoke, and everyone did a great job. The final speaker was the missionary. He was an impressive looking young man, and so I was a little puzzled when he said, "I'm sure a lot of you are surprised to see me here." I was equally taken aback also when everyone seemed to nod yes.

The missionary went on to explain that he had delayed going on his mission because he hadn't felt he had a testimony. When he told his parents that he didn't feel prepared to serve because he didn't have a testimony, his mother had responded by asking if he *wanted* a testimony. Of course he did, and so she suggested he read from the Book of Mormon every day for a week. She also recommended that at the end of the week he put Moroni's promise to the test. This young man went on to say that he had done just what his mother suggested but that nothing happened.

When he told his mother that he didn't feel any differently, she asked him, "When did you read?"

"Before going to bed."

"And, how long did you read?" she pressed.

"About five minutes, until I fell asleep."

"How would you feel," his mother had said, "if Heavenly Father only gave you the last five minutes of his day?"

Isn't that a great question? Anyway, then she suggested that he choose another time to read and offered to read with him. They chose to read after he got home from school, and instead of reading for five minutes, they would read for thirty minutes. After one week, the boy was to put Moroni's promise to the test again.

It was here that the young missionary looked down at the pulpit and paused. It was obvious he was trying to gain control of his emotions. When he finally did, he looked up and declared with great feeling that God had answered his prayer. He testified that he knew the Book of Mormon was true and that this is the true Church. He went on to say that he was excited to share his knowledge so that others could be as happy as he had become. He had tasted of the fruit. Isn't it interesting that the thing that made the difference was as simple as scheduling a favorable time to read?

You also probably noticed from that experience that he increased the time he read. Think about it, is five minutes long enough to spend with someone you love? Consider what President Howard W. Hunter encouraged us to do in this regard:

"Those who delve into the scriptural library . . . find that to understand requires more than casual reading or perusal—there must be concentrated study. It is certain that one who studies the scriptures every day accomplishes far more than one who devotes considerable time one day and then lets days go by before continuing. Not only should we study each day, but there should be a regular time set aside when we can concentrate without interference. . . .

"It would be ideal if an hour could be spent each day; but if that much cannot be had, a half hour on a regular basis would result in substantial accomplishment. A quarter of an hour is little time, but it is surprising how much enlightenment and knowledge can be acquired in a subject so meaningful. The important thing is to allow nothing else to ever interfere with our study" (*The Teachings of Howard W. Hunter* [1997], 52–53).

So, according to President Hunter, we need to devote at least fifteen minutes a day or more. Remember, at first that might not be easy. However, as you continue and partake more and more of God's love you will find that even an hour is sometimes not enough.

There is something else that I have found helpful. This principle comes from Doctrine and Covenants 33:16, which reads: "And the Book of Mormon and the holy scriptures are given of me for your instruction; and the power of my Spirit quickeneth all things."

Did you catch that last part? *The Spirit quickens all things.* Now be careful, the word *quicken* doesn't mean to make it go fast, although I admit when you read the scriptures with the Spirit the time does seem to fly. *Quicken* means to "make alive." That's right, when you read with the Spirit, the scriptures come alive. Have you ever felt that something you were reading was written just for you? There have been many times when I am reading that I feel almost like Heavenly Father and the Savior are speaking directly to me. Let me give you an example.

Early in my career as a seminary teacher, I was offered another job. It was something that I really wanted to do, but taking the job would mean that I would have to stop teaching seminary, which I also loved doing. For weeks I wrestled with the decision. Finally, after much thought and prayer and fasting, I read the following verse: "And now, as ye have begun to teach the word even so I would that ye should continue to teach; and I would that ye would be diligent and temperate in all things" (Alma 38:10).

This was advice Alma gave specifically to his son Shiblon, but when I read the passage, I felt it was for my benefit. That morning the scriptures came alive for me, and I knew that the Lord wanted me to continue teaching seminary.

Now, sometimes it may not be the exact wording, but the feeling we get as we read that makes the scriptures come alive. One young woman I knew related the following experience. It seems that one Friday afternoon her mom informed her that the young woman's uncle had passed away. The young woman didn't know her uncle that well, and so she wasn't too upset. However, she began to think about death and how temporary her life is, and this began to bother her.

That night she had arranged to go out with her friends and was anxious to talk to them about her feelings. Unfortunately, her friends showed little interest in the topic. She found herself in a somber mood and finally asked them to just take her home. By then she was feeling really confused and even a little scared.

After getting home, she went into her bedroom where she noticed her scriptures lying on her nightstand. She opened them, sat down on her bed, and began to read. As she related the experience, she said she couldn't remember exactly what she read. However, as she read, she had the most peaceful feeling come over her, and she knew that everything was okay. She knew that death was a part of God's plan and that he loved her.

That's the kind of thing that can and should happen when you read with the Spirit. Consider what Elder Dallin H. Oaks said concerning this: "Scripture reading may also lead to current revelation on whatever else the Lord wishes to communicate to the reader at that time. We do not overstate the point when we say that the scriptures can be a Urim and Thummim to assist each of us to receive personal revelation.

"Because we believe that scripture reading can help us receive revelation, we are encouraged to read the scriptures again and again. By this means, we obtain access to what our Heavenly Father would have us know and do in our personal lives today. That is one reason Latter-day Saints believe in *daily* scripture study" (*Ensign,* Jan. 1995, 8; emphasis in the original).

Just to recap, when you read under the influence of the Spirit, the scriptures can come alive, and you can receive revelation directed to you. So, what can you do to invite the Spirit to be with you when you read? There are lots of things. I will suggest just two.

First of all, I have found it very helpful to *pray* before I read the scriptures. In that prayer I usually ask for the Spirit to be with me as I read. In addition, I make sure to thank my Father in Heaven for the blessing of having the scriptures. Also, if there is anything that I am currently struggling with, I ask for guidance and direction.

Second, I have also found it useful to *ponder* what I read. President Marion G. Romney taught this concerning pondering: "As I have read the scriptures, I have been challenged by the word *ponder,* so frequently used in the Book of Mormon. The dictionary says that *ponder* means 'to weigh mentally, think deeply about, deliberate, meditate.' . . .

"*Pondering* is, in my feeling, a form of prayer. It has, at least, been an approach to the Spirit of the Lord on many occasions" (In Conference Report, Apr. 1973, 117; emphasis in original).

Pondering really pays off, but it is not easy. It takes real effort. Elder Jeffery R. Holland taught: "Reading which will give you any return on your investment will be an exercise . . . in which your mental and spiritual muscles are stretched and strengthened forever. . . . To ponder [the scriptures] suggests a slow and deliberate examination: indeed, there is no way to read the scriptures whimsically or superficially or quickly. They demand time, prayer, and honest meditation" (*Ensign,* Sept. 1976, 7).

Don't just read the words. Instead, consider deeply what the words *mean*. You can do this by asking questions. For example, Why didn't Nephi murmur like his brothers? or Why were the stripling warriors not killed when all around them men were dying? or how about, What did Joseph Smith do to get an answer to his prayers? One of the best questions you can ask is, How does this apply to me? Nephi called this "liken[ing]" the scriptures to ourselves (1 Nephi 19:23). As you read, the Spirit will lead you through the mists of darkness that surround us in this world (see 2 Nephi 32:5). When you ponder, you are really "feast[ing]" on the word (2 Nephi 32:3). You are satisfying that spiritual hunger you may not have realized you had.

Let me tie this all together with a personal note. My wife, Nancy, and I just had the opportunity of adopting a beautiful little boy. We have been unable to have children for several years, so you can imagine how excited we are. I can't even begin to tell you all the miracles that took place to bring this little boy into our hearts and home. Now, I know there will come a day when my son will have some questions about how he became a part of our family. It may even be a bit confusing for him. To help him, I have written down some things concerning how he came into our lives. One day he will be able to read how his dad felt the first time he saw him, how his father knew from the beginning that he was meant to be a member of this family, and especially how much his dad loves him.

In a very real way our Father in Heaven has done a similar thing for us. He knew that this life would not be easy. He also knew that we would have questions. So, he has given us the scriptures to answer those questions and to assure us that he loves us.

I love the scriptures, and I know you will come to love them, too, as you experience the happiness and joy that result from reading them daily under the influence of the Holy Spirit.

R. Scott Simmons served a mission to Cleveland, Ohio, then attended BYU and worked at the Missionary Training Center. He has taught seminary for eleven years and currently serves as a part-time instructor in the Department of Church History at BYU. He loves teaching the gospel, outdoor adventures, and spending time with his wife and son. He and his wife, Nancy, live in American Fork, Utah.

17

COME UNTO CHRIST: ACCEPTING THE SAVIOR'S INVITATION IN OUR LIVES

Richard Staples

We're having a party. You are invited to attend and the pleasure of your presence is requested.

Each of us enjoys getting an invitation to a party or to a friend's wedding reception. It is really nice to be wanted and thought of.

The Savior has extended to each of us a special invitation: "Come unto me, all ye that labour and are heavy laden, and I will give you rest. Take my yoke upon you, and learn of me; for I am meek and lowly in heart: and ye shall find rest unto your souls. For my yoke is easy, and my burden is light" (Matthew 11:28–30).

Christ's invitation to learn of him is not extended only to the lost or hurting. It is for everyone. It is comforting to have him say he will give us rest, for each of us is continually yearning for that peace only he can provide.

Peace comes in a variety of ways: through repentance, by enduring a lonely night where prayer brings peace to the soul, or making a correct but perhaps unpopular decision. What a blessing it is to have the Savior always wanting and ready to help comfort us. All we need to do is ASK.

As part of this invitation, the Savior says that his yoke is easy and his burden is light. Whenever I see the word *easy,* I reflect back to a time when I was coaching high school basketball. Several of my players were having a difficult time consistently making free throws. I pulled each of them aside and said, "Look, making a free throw is easy." Then I explained that if they would master the elements of free-throw shooting and apply them, making free throws would naturally follow. Those who listened and practiced, succeeded; those who chose to use their own ideas, struggled at times.

One young man, whose name we'll say was Mark, had a strong desire to improve his free throw shooting, and he listened very intently to my suggestions. Some time later, he was in a basketball game where we were ahead by one point with only about eight seconds to go. We were in our last time-out, setting up the last play to inbound the ball and run out the clock. The play was not designed to go to Mark, whose assignment was to be an outlet if necessary. The other team defended the out-of-bounds play quite well, and the ball was thrown to Mark, who was fouled immediately. About six seconds were left on the clock when Mark stepped up to the foul line.

With the crowd screaming against him, he momentarily forgot how easy it is to make a free throw. When he missed his first one, the other team called a time-out. That allowed me a chance to talk to Mark.

He was so worried about missing his free throw that on his way over to the sideline, he had his head down, and tears were streaming down his cheeks. The only thing I said to him was, "Remember what you have learned so far about how to shoot free throws, and you will make the next one." With Mark listening, I told the rest of the team, "After Mark makes his next free throw, this is what we will do. . . ." Well, he made his second free throw, much to his relief and my delight, and we won the game. Mark was a hero. The tears of sadness and discouragement turned to total excitement.

In this example, Mark relied on what he'd been taught and practiced. Once he remembered those principles and exercised faith in his abilities, making the free throw was easy. If we will rely on the Savior and accept his invitation to come unto him, he will make our burdens light and his yoke will be easy. He will help us do things we have trouble doing ourselves and possibly never thought we were capable of doing.

How do we know when we are truly trying to come unto him? What are some of the things we do to show that we are following him? Here are six areas to help us evaluate our progress in becoming more Christlike.

1. WE RECOGNIZE AND BELIEVE THAT WE ARE DAUGHTERS AND SONS OF GOD

"We are daughters of our Heavenly Father, who loves us and we love him" (Young Women theme). We must know, feel, and trust that we are loved by our Heavenly Father and that he will do what is best for us (see Proverbs 3:5–6). President Ezra Taft Benson said: "If we love God, do His will, and fear His judgment more than men's, we will have self-esteem" (*Ensign,* May 1989, 6).

2. "THEY HAD NO MORE DESIRE TO DO EVIL" (ALMA 19:33)

As we begin to accept the Savior's invitation to "Come unto me," we lose our desire to do evil and all we want to do is good. Our ambition is to do those things that please our Father in Heaven (see John 8:29). This contributes to his joy, and we receive happiness and peace of mind.

3. WE ARE CREATED TO HAVE "JOY" (2 NEPHI 2:25)

You are a happy person because you are doing the things of God. You have a positive outlook on life. I enjoy the message in a country-western song performed by Kenny Rogers. The song is about a little boy, who tries all day to hit a baseball, but without success. However, as he tries and fails, he keeps saying to himself that he is the best who's ever been. Finally, at the end of the day, he throws the baseball up one last time, swings once again, and misses. As he is walking home, he tells himself he is still the greatest, the best who's ever been. He just didn't know he could *pitch* like that! He turned a negative into a positive with the realization that he was such a good pitcher that he struck himself out all day long. What kind of attitude do we have toward the trials in our lives?

4. YOU ENJOY SERVING

This story about Elder Henry B. Eyring's father is a great example of Christlike service.

To appreciate this story, you have to realize that it occurred when Elder Eyring's father was nearly eighty and had bone cancer. He had bone cancer so badly in his hips that he could hardly move. The pain was great.

"Dad was the senior high councilor in his stake, and he had the responsibility for the welfare farm. An assignment was given to weed a field of onions, so Dad assigned himself to go work on the farm. He never told me how hard it was, but I have met several people who were with him that day. I talked to one of them on the phone, and he said that he was weeding in the row next to Dad through much of the day. He told me the same thing that others who were there that day have told me. He said that the pain was so great that Dad was pulling himself along on his stomach with his elbows. He couldn't kneel. The pain was too great for him to kneel. Everyone who has talked to me about that day has remarked how Dad smiled and laughed and talked happily with them as they worked in that field of onions.

"Now, this is the joke Dad told me on himself afterward. He said he was there at the end of the day. After all the work was finished and the onions were all weeded, someone said to him, 'Henry, good heavens! You didn't pull those weeds, did you? Those weeds were sprayed two days ago, and they were going to die anyway.'

"Dad just roared. He thought that was the funniest thing. He thought it was a great joke on himself. He had worked through the day in the wrong weeds. They had been sprayed and would have died anyway.

"When Dad told me this story, I knew how tough it was. So I asked him, 'Dad, how could you make a joke out of that? How could you take it so pleasantly?' He said something to me that I will never forget, and I hope you won't. He said, 'Hal, I wasn't there for the weeds.'

"Now, you'll be in an onion patch much of your life. So will I. It will be hard to see the powers of heaven magnifying us or our efforts. It may even be hard to see our work being of any value at all. And sometimes our work won't go well.

"But you didn't come for the weeds. You came for the Savior" (*To Draw Closer to God* [1997], 101–2).

When we serve others, what is our attitude? Do we have a Christlike willingness, or are we doing service reluctantly, just because we have to? If our desire is to accept the Savior's invitation to come unto him, our attitude in serving is one way to determine our current spiritual level. As we find ways to serve others, and in turn serve the Savior, we can seek the Lord's help to find joy and satisfaction in serving.

5. YOU DESIRE A CLOSER RELATIONSHIP WITH YOUR HEAVENLY FATHER

You choose to say your prayers morning and night. But you don't just pray. You do as President Harold B. Lee stated: "Learn to talk to God, . . . reaching right into the portals of our Father's holy dwelling place" (*The Teachings of Harold B. Lee* [1998], 125). As we begin to visualize actually speaking with our Father, our prayers will become more purposeful and focused. The same is true with scripture reading. If you can visualize actually being there, scripture reading will become more meaningful, and you will apply more directly Heavenly Father's teachings.

6. YOU WILL FORGIVE OTHERS

This is the last point. You don't hold grudges. As you begin coming unto Christ you find that your desire to forgive others increases. Forgiveness is the heart of the gospel. Christ taught it by example during his crucifixion as he cried, "Father, forgive them; for they know not what they do" (Luke 23:34). President Gordon B. Hinckley taught the following: "Teach our people always to forgive and forget. Get it behind them. We carry the cankering evil of memories of little things that destroy us and destroy our feelings, whereas with just a little turnaround, a little kindness, we could bestow blessings upon people (*Teachings of Gordon B. Hinckley* [1997], 230–31).

There is a great example in the scriptures of a people desiring to come unto Christ. It is found in the Book of Mormon and is the account of the resurrected Savior's visit to the Americas. After teaching the people for a period of time, he instructed them: "Therefore, go ye unto your homes, and ponder upon the things which I have said, and ask of the Father, in my name, that ye may understand, and prepare your minds for the morrow, and I come unto you again" (3 Nephi 17:3).

There are four points in this scripture, which will help us as we worship and read the scriptures.

"Go ye unto your homes." To help us understand the things our Heavenly Father wants us to learn, we must go to a quiet place and be alone so we can think. In other words, don't always be in a rush to be somewhere or to get things done.

"Ponder upon the things which I have said." Once we have found that quiet place, take some time to ponder the things that the Savior has given you and what you are learning.

"Ask of the Father, in my name, that ye may understand." If we prepare ourselves spiritually and then ask the Father for understanding, he will answer our prayers. A great example of this is the Prophet Joseph Smith when he asked the Father which church to join (Joseph Smith—History 1:18).

"Prepare your minds for the morrow, and I come unto you again." As we do all that is in our power, the Lord will be with us. What a wonderful promise. This also has reference to the sacramental prayers, where we are promised "that [we] may always have his Spirit to be with [us]" (D&C 20:77).

After the Savior shared this scripture with them, he saw that no one wanted him to leave. Having compassion on them, he said: "Have ye any that are sick among you? Bring them hither. Have ye any that . . . are afflicted in any manner? Bring them hither and I will heal them" (3 Nephi 17:7). Notice how the Savior invites us to come unto him so he can heal us of any affliction. President Howard W. Hunter said, "Whatever Jesus lays his hands upon lives. If Jesus lays his hands upon a marriage, it lives. If he is allowed to lay his hands on a family, it lives." (*Ensign,* Nov. 1979, 65). I know he can heal us of any affliction we have, whether it is physical or spiritual.

Through the Savior's Atonement, we can become totally clean. Allowing the Savior to touch our lives will bring us happiness, joy, and peace.

A few years ago my wife and I were able to visit the Holy Land. It was an awesome experience to walk where Jesus walked and see the places where he taught, performed miracles, made his atoning sacrifice, died, and was resurrected. One morning we had some free time to go and see some of the sights without the group, so we chose to go to the Garden of Gethsemane. What a beautiful place it is! Melinda and I were the only two people in the garden that morning, and we had some time to ponder sacred things. I cannot share with you all the events involved in that experience, but one of the things I was seeking was to know my standing with the Lord at that point in my life. I prayed fervently, and then it came to me—that quiet, calm, peaceful feeling that comes when you know it is right. I knew that I had been forgiven and that I stood approved by the Lord. What a wonderful feeling.

You can also have that same feeling by coming unto Christ and by letting him touch your life. You don't have to be in the Garden of Gethsemane to have such an experience. No matter where we choose to approach him, if we do so sincerely, he will respond to us. We can know with certainty that he loves us and that his atoning sacrifice and resurrection apply to us.

Shortly after I returned from my mission, my mother was diagnosed with cancer. All of my brothers and sisters were married by then, and I was the only one living at home with my parents. I was in total shock when the doctor told my mother that she had only six months to live, unless we could stop the cancer. We fasted and prayed for her, but the illness continued to progress. She had some good days, but she steadily got worse and worse.

Regrettably, I hadn't been too kind to my parents after my mission. Before my mission, I had a car, which was my pride and joy. While I was gone, my parents finished paying for it, and they also used it a lot. But they hadn't taken care of it the way I would have. For instance, the chrome wheels hadn't been polished and were corroded. The seat cover also had a big tear in it. Seeing the car in that condition upset me, and before we found out that Mom had cancer, I had complained to my parents about the way they had treated my car. Mom told me to get the seat fixed and offered to pay for it. I took care of the problems, and it was not very expensive; but my attitude and the way I acted were far from Christlike.

The night before my mother passed away, I purchased a beautiful red rose and took it to her in the hospital. When I walked into her room, I handed the rose to her and said, "Mom, do you know what this red rose means?"

She replied, "Yes, it means that you love me."

I said, "I sure do love you."

Those were the last words I spoke to my mother.

The next morning my father was at the hospital with my mom. At 6:45 A.M., before going out to milk our cows, I knelt in prayer. I prayed that if there was any way my mother could get better, to please help her do so; but if not, to please take her out of this life, so she wouldn't have to suffer any more. I was yearning for the rest and peace that Christ promised us when he said, "Come unto me, all ye that labour and are heavy laden, and I will give you rest" (Matthew 11:28). Within fifteen minutes of that prayer, I got a call from the hospital asking me to come down and informing me that Mom had just passed away. I took her passing to be an answer to my prayer.

Referring again to the time that my wife and I were in Jerusalem, we were able to visit the tomb of the resurrected Lord. There was a sign on the entrance to the tomb with this inscription: "He is not here: for he is risen" (Matthew 28:6). As I considered that statement, I felt a confirming Spirit. I knew then and I know now that I will see my mother once again. I can't wait to have my children sit on Grandma's lap and feel her warm embrace. What a wonderful feeling and thought: we will all enjoy her presence because of the Savior and his resurrection.

As we strive to do his will and come unto him, we are able to enjoy the blessings that he has for each of us. I testify that as you set goals for accomplishing the task of coming unto Christ and dedicate your life to him and his service, you will find great rewards. I know that our Father hears and answers prayers and that he is just waiting for you to draw closer to him. The blessings are there. What a wonderful group of young people we have today. I pray for each of you, that you will find success in completing your journey through life and make it back to the celestial kingdom with our Father.

Richard Staples was born and raised in Coalville, Utah. The youngest of seven children, he served a full-time mission in the Tennessee Nashville Mission. He graduated from Brigham Young University with a bachelor's degree in Education and later received a master's degree from Utah State University. Brother Staples married Melinda Reed in the Manti Temple, and they have six children—four boys and two girls. He taught seminary for thirteen years and currently serves as a Church Educational System coordinator in Marysville, California, where he directs institute and supervises three stakes of early morning seminary

18

WHAT IN THE WORLD DOES THE WORLD BELIEVE?

Brad Wilcox

The world recently celebrated the arrival of the six billionth person now living on the planet. Look what Adam and Eve started! Look what Noah and his wife *restarted!* That's quite a posterity. However, very few of the great-great-great-great-great- (you get the picture) grandchildren of those ancient patriarchs are being true to the faith that their original parents cherished. In fact, only about one in every six hundred people is a member of The Church of Jesus Christ of Latter-day Saints in today's world.

What do the rest of our brothers and sisters believe? Some are Christians, but the majority live by other beliefs. Where did those religions come from? As The Church of Jesus Christ of Latter-day Saints becomes increasingly international and young people prepare to serve missions around the globe, it is important that we understand something about the religious beliefs found in the world.

There are many different religions and churches. Native Americans alone have over five hundred distinct religious traditions. African tribal religions number in the thousands. In addition to these groups, the National Geographic Society lists eight prominent world religions: Hinduism, Buddhism, Islamism, Shintoism, Taoism, Confucianism, Judaism, and Christianity. The following brief descriptions of each group's history and beliefs are meant to serve only as introductions, not as complete overviews.

HINDUISM

Have you ever heard someone speak of "sacred cows"? Most Hindus do not eat meat because of their respect for all forms of life. Cows are revered by Hindus because they represent a path to unity with the great cosmic force or spirit of the universe (Brahma).

The word *Hindu* is derived from *Indus,* the name of a valley and a river in India where people lived about 2500 B.C. About 1,000 years later, a group of fair-skinned Aryans invaded India from the north. The beginnings of Hinduism are usually traced to when the Aryans' tribal religion mixed with local customs. Hindus believe in many gods. The god Krishna is the focus of the Hindu sect Hare Krishna. The god Vishnu is said to have come on various occasions in a variety of forms to help the people. Once he came as a fish to warn of a flood, another time as a warrior to help them do battle. The sacred writings of the Hindus are recorded in four books called the Vedas.

Faithful Hindus have shrines in their homes where they light lamps, burn incense, pray, and leave offerings of fruit and flowers to please the gods. In an effort to open their minds to truth, Hindus spend much time meditating. Hindus believe in reincarnation, or being born and reborn many times. If they are wicked, they will be punished in their next lives, but if they are good, they will be rewarded by being reborn into better circumstances. This is called the law of karma.

BUDDHISM

About five hundred years before Christ, a prince in India named Siddhartha Gautama sat beneath a bodhi tree and received a vision of life's deeper meaning. This moment marked the end of a six-year search for wisdom during which he had left his home, lived in a forest, and listened to many religious teachers. After experiencing this vision or epiphany, the prince was known as "the enlightened one," or Buddha. My father, who was stationed in India during World War II, has photographs of himself standing in front of some of the many statues of Buddha that are found throughout that country.

Followers of Buddha seek enlightenment by avoiding extremes, respecting all living things, and learning to focus their minds through meditation. Although Buddhists reject some Hindu teachings, the faiths are quite similar. Like Hindus, Buddhists believe people are born and reborn many different times until they reach Nirvana—a condition of perfect peace and harmony with all things. Sacred symbols include the bodhi tree and the lotus flower, which remind them that they can remain clean even if they are placed in a muddy pond.

ISLAMISM

The Old Testament tells of Abraham sending Hagar and their son, Ishmael, into the desert. Once their provisions were gone, the two would have faced certain death had God not intervened by sending an angel to show them a well of water and to give them a promise that Ishmael would father a great nation (see Genesis 16). The large city of Mecca now stands over the supposed location of that well in today's Saudi Arabia. Faithful Muslims strive to travel (make a pilgrimage) there at least once during their lives.

Approximately 2,500 years after Hagar and Ishmael lived, a merchant in Mecca named Muhammad did not approve of the worshipping of idols that was taking place all around him. Seeking inspiration, he went to a cave where he prayed for hours. Muslims believe that Muhammad's prayer was answered by an angel who told him that there was only one God—Allah—and that Muhammad was to be Allah's messenger to the world. The messages Muhammad received are recorded in a sacred book called the Koran. Those who believe Muhammad was a prophet are called Muslims, but their religion is called Islamism, meaning "to surrender or submit to Allah." Moons and stars are sacred symbols that appear on the tops of churches (mosques) and even on the flags of many Middle Eastern countries.

Five times a day, faithful Muslims declare in prayer their belief that Allah is God and Muhammad is his prophet. They go to a mosque every Friday, help the poor, aspire to live good lives, and fast during their month of Ramadan. When I was a child, my family lived in Ethiopia, Africa. I remember helping my mom prepare food for a group of Muslim men who were working on our home. They politely refused Mom's offer, saying, "Ramadan. Ramadan." Muslims follow a strict code of ethics and morality as they seek protection against Satan and walk the path to Allah.

SHINTOISM

Shintoism is the predominant religion in Japan, where the rising sun is symbolic of the beginning of life. *Shinto* means "way of the gods," and Shintoists believe in many gods *(kami)* who have supernatural powers to bless human lives. Peace and protection result from pleasing these gods, so believers offer food and other gifts in sacred shrines. Worship also includes many cleansing rituals. When I had the opportunity of visiting Japan, I saw a number of beautiful shrines where Shintoists would burn incense and then wave the smoke toward themselves. They would then touch their ears, eyes, noses, mouths, and necks in a symbolic cleansing.

There is no known founder of Shintoism, which emerged about the same time as Hinduism. Shintoists focus on the here and now rather than on the hereafter. They devote their energies to enjoying and improving what is good in this life. Priests bless crops and market places and participate in festivals and ceremonies to celebrate special times such as the harvest, birth, the coming of age, and marriage.

TAOISM

About the same time that Lehi and his family were leaving Jerusalem and journeying toward the promised land (600 B.C.), there was a librarian named Lao-tzu living in China. He had become disenchanted with the emperor and his court. Lao-tzu decided to leave the city and live in the country, but as he left through the city gates, the guards asked him to teach them. His words to the guards became part of a book of wisdom called the Tao Te Ching, and Lao-tzu became the founder of Taoism. Lao-tzu taught that Tao (meaning "the way") is an unchanging essence and that everything has its opposite. From these opposing forces (the yin and the yang) comes the rhythm of life.

Faithful Taoists believe there is an energy inside every living thing *(ch'i),* which holds the secret to everlasting life. Believers do daily breathing exercises in an effort to tap into that energy. They also believe the world is full of magical spirits, who can heal and purify people. Priests perform ceremonies to help believers become less preoccupied with themselves, seeking instead harmony with nature.

CONFUCIANISM

About one hundred years after Lao-tzu began teaching, Confucius was born. As he matured, he developed a dislike of the violence, greed, and evil he saw all around him. He studied great philosophies of the past and then began to travel around China, teaching people to be kind and to control their anger. He told them to honor their parents and respect their leaders. His simple teachings influenced millions. His words were recorded in books that were studied and memorized. When Confucius died, many temples were built to his memory. Today, people visit these temples to pay tribute to this wise man and to the other great teachers who followed in his tradition.

Confucianism includes ceremonies full of art, dance, and music, as well as animal sacrifice. When a boy becomes a man or when a girl is engaged to be married, the individual is given new clothes and a new name. The crane bird is their symbol of strength and long life.

JUDAISM

The Old Testament records that Abraham was the father of Isaac, who was the father of Jacob. Jacob's name was later changed to Israel (see Genesis 35:10), and he had twelve sons, one of whom was Judah. It is from this great-grandson of Abraham that the Jews descend.

Jews reverence the words of ancient prophets, particularly Moses. These writings are compiled in the Torah (the first five books of the Old Testament) and the Talmud (sixty-three books interpreting and explaining the Torah). In these writings Jews find their rules for living, including the Ten Commandments. Jews meet in buildings called synagogues.

When a Jewish boy reaches the age of thirteen, he can become a member of the congregation by reading from the Torah in Hebrew. This special service is called a bar mitzvah. The six-sided star of (King) David is a symbol associated with the Jews, along with the seven- (or nine-) pronged candlestick (menorah), which is used during religious rites and celebrations that remind the Jews of God's promises to Abraham and of the many miracles God has performed to deliver and protect the Israelite people.

I once met a university student who was a devout Jew but who didn't dress in the traditional way often depicted in the movies. He explained that some Jews are Orthodox, others are Conservative, and still others refer to themselves as Reformed. "Each group does things differently," he said. "But regardless of the denomination, we all await the coming of the Messiah who will redeem our people and the world."

CHRISTIANITY

Those who profess to be Christians believe that Jesus of Nazareth was the Messiah or Christ, whom the Jews are still awaiting. Most Christians believe in the divinity of Christ, that he is the Son of God born to Mary, his virgin mother. Christians also believe that by following Jesus' perfect example and teachings, they can find happiness and peace in this life and eternal life in the next. Christians believe in the Old Testament, but add to it the New Testament, which documents the life and words of Jesus and of the disciples who followed him. The New Testament records that Jesus was killed by Roman soldiers who nailed him to a cross—the most widely recognized symbol of Christianity throughout the world.

Most Christians believe that three days after his crucifixion, Jesus Christ rose from the dead, thus breaking the bands of death and offering a resurrection to all. Everyone who believes and accepts Jesus Christ can find forgiveness for sins through the Savior's Atonement and can ultimately live eternally with God.

Christianity is perhaps the most fractured of the world's faiths. After Jesus' death, the apostles were ultimately killed, and early Christians were persecuted mercilessly. Then Constantine the Great experienced a miraculous conversion in 312 A.D. and made Christianity the official religion of his entire empire. Roman Catholics (from the Greek word *katholikos,* meaning "universal") believe theirs is the universal Christian church organized by Jesus and that Christ's apostle Peter was the first pope. However, many principles and practices of the Catholic Church are at odds with those in Christ's original Church. This has led many groups through the years to split away from the Catholics.

The Copts (Coptic Christians) were the first to break away. These people lived primarily in Egypt and Ethiopia. I vividly remember, as a child growing up in Ethiopia, seeing the Coptic crosses, churches, symbols, and ceremonies. I remember seeing paintings of the birth of Christ and other familiar scenes from his life in which all the people in the painting were African.

The next group to break away from the Roman Catholics was a gathering of Christians living in what today is Turkey and neighboring countries. Their differences with the Catholic Church, both in language and in theology, proved irreconcilable. Those in the east spoke Greek, while Rome used Latin. Among other things, the rival groups argued over the nature of God and the Godhead and about the authority vested in the pope. Finally, there was a break, and the Eastern Orthodox Church was formed.

In the early 1500s a German monk named Martin Luther became troubled by some of the practices of the Catholic Church, such as selling indulgences (a practice that provided for forgiveness of sins in advance, in return for the payment of money to the church). Luther published a list of ninety-five complaints, and this protest launched the Protestant movement. Others soon joined in the attempt to reform Christianity.

One such person was John Calvin, who separated from the Catholics and the Lutherans to organize a church in Switzerland, which would be led by a group of church members rather than by popes or bishops. These men were called presbyters (elders), and the Presbyterian Church was born. Later, John Knox took Calvin's ideas to Scotland, where in 1560, Presbyterianism was declared the state religion. In the early 1600s, there were various movements away from Calvinism, resulting in the formation of such churches as the Reformed Protestants, the Disciples of Christ, the Churches of Christ, and the Baptists who were led by Roger Williams.

When King Henry VIII of England wanted to divorce his wife, and the Catholic Church refused him permission, the king created the Church of England (Anglican) and decreed that British kings and queens would lead the church and appoint bishops. At the end of the American Revolution, colonists who were members of the Church of England but who were no longer subject to the British crown began to appoint their own bishops, and the American version of the Anglican Church became known as the Episcopalian Church (*episkopos* means "bishop" in Greek). The United Church of Christ and the Methodists later broke away from the Anglican community. The Methodists, led by John Wesley, got their name because they were so methodical in their discipleship. Later still, the Pentecostal Assemblies (named for the day of Pentecost mentioned in the New Testament) broke away from the Methodists.

In the 1600s an Englishman named George Fox organized The Religious Society of Friends, nicknamed the Quakers because they taught that all men would quake in the presence of God. In 1694 a Swiss farmer named Jacob Ammann felt that large, ornate churches and wealthy lifestyles were not in harmony with the simple life led by Jesus. His followers became the Amish. Both groups fled persecution and sought religious freedom in America.

In fact, the religious freedom guaranteed in the Constitution of the United States served as the seedbed for many new Christian faiths, including the Seventh-Day Adventists, Christian Scientists, and Unitarians in the early 1800s and the Jehovah's Witnesses in the early 1900s.

Of special significance to us is a religious movement that began in the early 1800s in upstate New York, which was completely unlike any other. This was not just the creation of a new church or the reformation of an existing church; it was the *restoration* of *the* Church—the very Church organized by Christ when he lived on the earth, founded on the eternal principles and doctrines and practices revealed by God to Adam, Noah, and all ancient prophets. On April 6, 1830, having been authorized by heavenly messengers and a divine appointment, Joseph Smith organized The Church of Jesus Christ of Latter-day Saints. It was an event that had long been prophesied and one that would impact the whole world and everyone who had ever lived upon it.

What does all this mean to us? As Christians? As Latter-day Saints? Perhaps an experience from my father-in-law's personal history can offer some insight. My father-in-law, Leroy Gunnell, was teaching English at the Air Force Academy in Colorado during the Vietnam War. Each class had a section leader, who was responsible for calling the class to attention and reporting, "All present and accounted for, Sir." One day the section leader gave his usual report but then added, "Sir, we would rather not discuss English today."

My father-in-law laughed. "That doesn't surprise me," he said. "What would you like to discuss?"

"Religion, Sir."

The section leader's response caught Dad off guard. Was the young man serious? Or had he and his classmates learned that Dad was serving as a bishop in the local LDS ward? Were they just teasing him or trying to bait him? He searched the room for any sign of snickering. There was none. The cadets were sincere. The Vietnam War was in full swing. Many of their former classmates had died, and it would not be long before they would be facing their own dangerous assignments. They were nervous and concerned. Dad said, "All right. Put your books away and let's discuss religion." He nodded to the section leader, "Why don't you start."

The section leader explained that he had been raised a Catholic but now had serious doubts about his religion, about the existence of God, about why he should live a moral life at all. "I just don't know what I believe any more," he said. "The only reason I'm a Christian is because I happened to born where I was born. If I had been born in India, I would probably be a Hindu or Buddhist. If I had been born in Japan, I would probably be a Shintoist."

Another young man said he had been raised in a conservative Jewish home. He expressed many of the same doubts and uncertainties as the first. Others suggested that perhaps religion was just manmade and that if there were a higher power it wasn't going to be found in any organized church. Still others said that all religions were just parallel ways to reach the same God, who manifests himself differently to different cultures throughout the earth. One young man said, "No one can claim that one religion is more right or true or any better than another. They are all the same."

My father-in-law listened as each of the cadets had the opportunity to express his belief or disbelief. Dad says, "It was one of the most heartfelt, soul-baring times I have ever witnessed. It was amazing to realize how desperately most of these young men wanted something to believe in—something that would satisfy their deepest spiritual needs."

When about ten minutes remained in the class period, Dad took the opportunity to sum up. He said, "I appreciate what you've shared with me. I know how troubling it can be when you feel the foundations of your faith are being torn away. However, before we end class I would like you to consider a few questions. First of all, which of the founders of the world's major religions declared himself to be divine? Buddha did not. Muhammad did not. Nor did Lao-tzu, Confucius, Abraham, or Moses. Only one religious leader made such a claim, then backed it up by the way he lived, the things he taught, and the miracles he performed. That was Jesus Christ."

The young men were silent and pensive. Dad continued, "Do you know any religious leader of any faith who not only claimed the power to be able to suffer and atone for the sins of the world, but was willing to do so? Did Buddha or Muhammad? Did the founders of Hinduism or Shintoism? No, the only one who claimed such a thing was Jesus Christ.

"Do you know any religious leader who claimed to have power over life and death? Did any claim to resurrect himself? Only Jesus made that claim and then appeared to his disciples as a resurrected being. I want you to realize that all the religions of the world are not the same."

Class was almost over. My father-in-law felt that the young men had appreciated his willingness to listen to their doubts and concerns. Before they left, Dad said to them, "Now before you young men give up having faith in God, I challenge you to investigate thoroughly the message of Christianity. And before you get too discouraged with all the differences found among Christian churches, I want you to know that there is additional truth on the earth today for those willing to search for it."

I am grateful for the encouragement and insight my father-in-law gave to those young cadets during the Vietnam War. Truly, there is good to be found in all of the world's religions, and they are similar in ways that should bind us together in tolerance and love. However, salvation (resurrection and eternal life) is found only through Jesus Christ (see John 14:6), and the fullness of his gospel and the authority to perform the saving ordinances resides in only one church—the only church that offers the fullness of the gospel to everyone through missionary work and temple work—The Church of Jesus Christ of Latter-day Saints.

How blessed we are to have testimonies of God the Eternal Father, his Son Jesus Christ, and the Holy Ghost. How blessed we are to have testimonies of Christ's Atonement and his role as Savior and Redeemer. How blessed we are to have testimonies of the restoration of the gospel in these last days. Regardless of what six billion people on the earth now believe, one day every knee shall bow and every tongue confess that Jesus is the Christ, the holy Messiah (see D&C 88:104), and it will be universally known that he did in fact restore his Church through the Prophet Joseph Smith. Of these things I testify.

Brad Wilcox enjoys teaching future teachers in the David O. McKay School of Education at Brigham Young University, where he also directs the Mexico Student Teaching Program and the Guatemala Internships. He served his mission in Chile and is married and has four children. He loves pepperoni pizza, peanut M&Ms, and driving with the volume of his car stereo turned way up (listening to the EFY tapes, of course). He currently serves as bishop of the BYU 138th Ward.

Note: The sketches of world religions in this chapter are based primarily on information found in three books: A World of Faith *by Peggy Fletcher Stack and Kathleen Peterson (Signature Books, 1998);* The World's Religions, *2d ed. by Ninian Smart (Cambridge University Press, 1998); and* Great Religions of the World *(National Geographic Society, 1971).*

19

FOLLOW THE BRETHREN

Randal A. Wright

Through personal experience I have learned that the General Authorities of the Church, both past and present, are inspired of God. I have made it a practice in my life to record the experiences that remind me that this principle is true. I would like to share just a few of them with you, in the hope you will be convinced that to follow the leaders of our Church is the best policy.

Marion G. Romney: "You can make every decision in your life correctly if you can learn to follow the guidance of the Holy Spirit" (in Conference Report, Oct. 1961, 60).

It was a beautiful summer day, and my friends and I were looking forward to a fun afternoon of water skiing. We had a powerful boat to pull us down the river, but our skis left a little to be desired. One was a slalom ski, the other a regular ski for the right foot. Because one of the skis was nearly a foot longer than the other, we had a little harder time than usual getting up as the boat tugged on our towrope. But we were having a really good time, and I was proud of myself for overcoming the inconvenience of the mismatched skis, especially since I had been water skiing only a few times in my life.

As the boat pulled me down the river, we passed a ski jump ramp owned by a local ski club. Friends in the boat began coaxing me to attempt the jump. As Jim, the driver, circled past the ramp several times, I resisted the challenge. I kept thinking, *Yeah, right, I barely know how to ski. I'm sure not going over any ski ramp!*

But they continued to encourage me to jump, employing a few words that implied that maybe I was afraid. They had that part right. The thought of making that jump scared me to death! However, before long another thought crossed my mind—*You know, it'd be really cool to be the only one brave enough to go over the jump.* When I signaled Jim to pull me toward the jump, a cheer went up from my friends in the boat. I could sense their surprise that I would really go through with it.

As I neared the ramp, I felt almost confident that I could succeed at what I was about to do. I took pleasure also in knowing I would be a hero of sorts to the wimps in the boat because of the feat I was about to accomplish.

I was ready as we drew closer to the jump, but the moment my skis hit the ramp, I realized I was in trouble. Jumping skis don't have rudders on the bottom, but the two mismatched ones I was wearing did. And yet, with all the scraping and wobbling that occurred as I was dragged up the ramp, I somehow managed to stay upright. I actually cleared the end of the ramp standing up, and as I descended toward the water, I heard the cheers from my friends in the boat. I felt as though I had just won a world championship.

I was so excited about clearing the end of the ramp, though, that I forgot to concentrate on my landing. Later I learned that when you land after jumping, it's essential to keep the tips of your skis pointed slightly upward. Mine, according to those in the boat, were pointed more or less straight down. I remember hitting the water at a high rate of speed. The longer ski snagged the water first, and my forward motion stopped almost immediately. When I slammed into the water, it was as though I'd done a bellyflop off a fifty-foot high dive. I hit the water so hard that I seriously thought I would lose my eyesight, and the skin on the front of my body turned a bright red, from my head to my feet. Of course, once they determined that I wasn't dead, my friends thought it was hilarious. The fact is, I was very lucky not to be seriously hurt.

Others who have caved into the pressures brought by the crowd have not been so lucky. We need to be careful not to let our desire to be accepted by friends lead us into making bad decisions. We should study things out and think of the possible consequences before acting and then follow the whisperings of the Spirit to make correct decisions.

Joseph Smith: "Our missionaries are going forth to different nations, and . . . the Standard of Truth has been erected; no unhallowed hand can stop the work from progressing; persecutions may rage, mobs may combine, armies may assemble, calumny may defame, but the truth of God will go forth boldly, nobly, and independent, till it has penetrated every continent, visited every clime, swept every country, and sounded in every ear, till the purposes of God shall be accomplished, and the Great Jehovah shall say the work is done" (*History of the Church,* 4:540).

Whenever I hear the word *Olympics,* my mind often returns to 1972. My brother and I were students at Brigham Young University that year and were excited because Bubba, an athlete from our home area in Texas, was competing in the boxing competition. Although boxing can be a brutal sport, we felt an obligation to follow a young man from our area. Bubba was a five-time Texas State Golden Gloves boxing champion, and some predicted that he would win the gold medal in the Olympics that year. We were disappointed when our local boxer was eliminated in the first round of the competition. In fact, going into the gold medal round, the USA team had only one boxer left, Ray Seales, from Washington state. His nickname was "Sugar Ray" Seales.

The fighters from the communist nations were dominating boxing that year. Since Seales was the only boxer from the United States to compete for the gold, my brother and I decided to watch the match. Before the bout started, they showed highlights of some of the fights Sugar Ray's opponent had won. He was from Bulgaria, and his name was Angel Anghelov. He had dominated his previous opponents and was heavily favored to win the gold medal.

We had never seen Ray Seales box before and didn't know anything about him. When he was interviewed before the match and asked what he thought his chances were of winning the gold, his response made us laugh. Standing six feet tall and weighing only 112 pounds, he didn't look much like a boxer. He also had an unusually high-pitched voice. Still a teenager, Ray Seales was a boy who had been matched against a man. My brother and I wrote him off as having no chance against the more experienced Bulgarian.

When asked about his opponent, Seales confidently replied, "Well, he's good, but I think I can beat him with my superior boxing ability." When he said that, my brother and I began to laugh even harder. His prediction seemed foolish, and we seriously worried about him getting hurt. With the communist nations' boxers having won gold medals in seven out of eight fights, the Bulgarian boxer was a heavy favorite to win. It appeared certain that the USA would go home without any gold medals in boxing.

The first round began, and it went just as I expected. As predicted, the Bulgarian boxer completely dominated Ray Seales. In the second round, however, Sugar Ray discovered that he had at least one thing in his favor. His arms were much longer than his opponent's. He began using those long arms to flick jabs into his opponent's face. Soon he even began to score some points against the Bulgarian. Sensing what might be possible, my brother and I got down on the floor to cheer for our boxer. I usually pull for the underdog anyway, but since this was an American, I felt doubly justified. By the third round, Ray Seales discovered the power he really had and began to use it. When the judges' decision was announced, Ray Seales was named the winner, and the United States had its only gold medal in boxing for that Olympics. The unbelievable turn of events shocked the boxing experts.

There are some similarities between what happened to Ray Seales and the way the gospel has come forth in the last days. In one corner we have Satan and his formidable forces. Throughout the world's history, they've had unbelievable success in their battle to turn mankind to sin. Those evil forces have only lost a few rounds but have never really lost an entire fight. In the other corner we have The Church of Jesus Christ of Latter-day-Saints. In the early years of its existence, the Church was misjudged by many and given no chance of surviving, let alone winning. Like Ray Seales, who alone had confidence in what he could do, Joseph Smith was at first the only one who understood the destiny of the little church he had restored. The Prophet's enemies declared he had no chance against such a formidable foe.

Even members of the Church sometimes lose heart, wondering if the gospel can actually prevail in the face of so much evil and corruption as exists in the world. We must never forget, however, that in the end, the forces of the Great Jehovah will come out the winner. Perhaps we're in the second round and have begun to discover some of our strengths. Like Ray Seales, we need to have confidence that we can ultimately win the final battle—that as Joseph Smith prophesied, the gospel of Jesus Christ will, in the end, overcome the forces of evil.

Ezra Taft Benson: "From simple trials to our

Gethsemanes, prayer can put us in touch with God, our greatest source of comfort and counsel" (in Conference Report, Oct. 1974, 91).

While speaking at a youth conference in Ohio, I met a young LDS athlete who had played on a nationally ranked high school football team the previous fall. During the testimony meeting, this outstanding young man shared a special experience he had had with prayer.

Traveling on the bus to the state championship game, which his team was favored to win, he was thinking about how much he had enjoyed being a member of that team. As he pondered, he closed his eyes and offered a silent prayer of gratitude. During the prayer, the Spirit whispered to him that his team would lose the football game that day, but that he needn't be upset because he had been a great example to his team members. In his testimony, he said it had been a comfort to him to know that he was a winner in Heavenly Father's eyes, no matter the score of the game.

As the Spirit whispered to him, he experienced a feeling of peace and an overwhelming sense of love for everyone. Tears of joy began to roll down his cheeks, and when he opened his eyes, he saw several of his teammates looking at him. When they asked him what was wrong, he said "Nothing," that he was just thinking. They naturally assumed he was nervous about the big game they were about to play. In reality, he said, he had never been more calm in his life.

He and his teammates played as hard as they could, but the state championship went to the opposing team. After the game, almost all his teammates were very upset, but this young LDS athlete didn't shed a tear. He said he felt a sense of peace and love like never before. He quickly went to members of the opposing team and told them how well they had played and congratulated them on their victory.

Then he joined his teammates and did his best to lift their sagging spirits.

His testimony was that losing the state championship that day was one of the greatest experiences of his life because he learned for himself that Heavenly Father answers prayers and that the Spirit can bring great peace and comfort in times of need. We can face and overcome great disappointments in life if we have the Spirit with us.

David O. McKay: "So live, then, that each day will find you conscious of having willfully made no person unhappy" ("*Something Higher than Self,*" Brigham Young University *Speeches of the Year* [1966], 14).

Several years ago I attended a class on kindness given by two popular youth speakers. After the presentation, I noticed a young man (I'll call Trent) sitting by himself after everyone else had left. He was obviously very upset about something. The two speakers and I asked him if we could be of assistance. After a long hesitation, he opened up and told us what had happened.

We learned that Trent had been very popular in his high school, where he was one of only a few LDS students. Just prior to his school's prom, he was invited by a young woman (I'll call Lori) to be her date. Lori was a member of his ward, and he had a strong feeling that he ought to accept the date. But Lori wasn't as pretty as some of the other girls at school, and definitely not pretty enough to be seen with at the prom. So he turned her down.

Later on, one of the "cute" girls invited Trent to go to the dance with her, but he felt guilty accepting a date with her after turning down Lori, so he just stayed home that night.

During the class, while the speaker was talking about being kind to others, it came home to Trent how unkind he had been to Lori. He told us that months later, his bishop had told him that prior to the prom, Lori had complained to the bishop that she didn't feel accepted by the boys in the ward. The bishop had encouraged her to ask one of the priests in the ward to the prom. She had ended up asking two, but both had turned her down.

Because the LDS boys had turned her down, Lori told her parents that she had decided to ask a non-LDS boy to the dance. Admiring Trent and believing that he wouldn't turn their daughter down, they convinced Lori that rather than ask a nonmember, she should call Trent. She did so, but the unhappy boy sitting before us had said no.

Lori gave up on the priests at that point and asked the non-LDS boy to be her date. He quickly accepted, and they soon began dating steadily. Within a short time she got pregnant out of wedlock.

At first Trent felt no responsibility for what had happened to Lori. However, attending the class on kindness had reminded him of the role he had played. He wondered if he could have made a difference and was feeling tremendous guilt for not being more kind to her. Through his tears, he said, "If I had just treated her with respect and built her up, this might have never happened."

Who knows if that is true? It's impossible to say. The point is, Trent had an opportunity to be kind to someone who needed a friend. Imagine the difference it might have made in both their lives if he had acted on the prompting he received and responded in a kind way to Lori's invitation.

We should worry more about looking good to Heavenly Father than looking good to our peers.

Ezra Taft Benson: "One who is kind is sympathetic and gentle with others. He is considerate of others' feelings and courteous in his behavior. He has a helpful nature. Kindness pardons others' weaknesses and faults. Kindness is extended to all—to the aged and the young, to animals, to those low of stations as well as the high" (*Ensign,* Nov. 1986, 47).

As the bishop of our ward, I had some concern when I

found out that the priests had been put in charge of the skit for our ward camp-out. That evening as Jeff came out leading our teenage daughter Naomi with a towel over her head, I knew that I was wise to have been concerned.

Jeff said, "What we have here is the world's ugliest woman. If anyone can look at her for ten seconds, we'll give you ten dollars. Who would like to try?" A couple of ward members held up their hands. These people had obviously been coached in what was about to happen and were in on the joke.

The first person stepped to Naomi's side and briefly peeked under the towel. With a look of horror on his face, he shouted, "She's too ugly! I can't look at her!" He quickly turned away.

Jeff then commented that this woman was *so* ugly that he'd give someone *fifty dollars* if they could look at her for ten seconds. Another previously arranged volunteer was called out of the audience. The towel was slightly raised again, but after taking one glance at Naomi, the person screeched and quickly fled.

I knew we should have put some adults in charge of the skits. Jeff cried out, "This woman is *so* ugly that we will give anyone *one hundred dollars* if they can look at her for ten seconds." Jeff then called on one of my counselors in the bishopric to make his attempt to look at her face. I could tell as he slowly walked toward the front that Brother Penrod was *not* in on the joke and that he wasn't sure what he was expected to do. However, he was a good sport and wanted to help make the priest's skit successful. Just like the two previous participants, he lifted a corner of the towel and was about to yell, when suddenly our daughter screamed at the top of her lungs, "He's too ugly!" and ran off, leaving him holding the towel in his hands. Of course, the ward members thought it was hilarious. And Brother Penrod took it all in stride, so I guess it turned out okay.

After the program ended, the priests and Laurels were standing in a group, talking about how they had tricked Brother Penrod. Naomi noticed one of the eleven-year-old girls in our ward standing close by, looking as though she wanted to say something. This young girl had a severe speech impediment.

When Naomi turned to talk to her, the little girl said, "Ewe not u-u-gly, ewe pritty!" Obviously not understanding the skit, she felt a need to build Naomi up after she thought that other ward members had made fun of her. She probably knew what it felt like to be the source of ridicule and didn't want anyone else to go through the same experience.

We need to be aware of those around us and be sensitive and kind to those who may be struggling. Things we think we see may be far different than the way we perceive them.

H. Burke Peterson: "If our words are not consistent with our actions, they will never be heard above the thunder of our deeds" (*Ensign,* Nov. 1982, 43).

A few years ago I spoke at a Know Your Religion class in Mesa, Arizona, on a Friday night. Earlier in the day, at the request of a good friend, I had spoken to the students at a high school seminary in Chandler. My topic was the importance of being a good example.

That night after the Know Your Religion class, I decided to go see a movie that several people had highly recommended. I figure a good movie comes along about every ten years, so I didn't want to miss it. I checked a local paper and found that it was playing at a theater in Tempe. As I pulled into the theater parking lot, I noticed that all the movies were R-rated except the PG one that I had come to see.

As I was walking to the ticket booth, I saw a poster for a widely advertised, R-rated movie that was being highly acclaimed by the critics. For a moment the thought passed through my mind: *You are in Tempe, Arizona, and you don't know one person here. No one will ever know which movie you go to.* Immediately, another thought came to mind: *Oh, yeah? At least two people will know. My Heavenly Father will know and so will I.*

When it was my turn to buy a ticket, the teenage worker asked what movie I wanted to see. I told him that I wanted to see the PG-rated one. When I said that, the young man smiled, as though he approved of my choice. I couldn't help wondering why he would care which movie I saw that night.

As he handed me my ticket, he said, "Thanks, Brother Wright."

Startled, I asked him how he knew who I was. He said he had been there when I gave my talk to the seminary students earlier that day—a talk on the importance of being a good example.

I experienced a tremendous feeling of relief. I thanked my Heavenly Father for helping me have the courage to resist temptation. I couldn't help but think of how it might have affected that teenage seminary student had I chosen the other movie. We need to be an example at all times and in all places.

Marvin J. Ashton: "The desire to achieve has been placed in us by a loving Creator who honors our free agency but nonetheless beckons to us to do well" (*Ensign*, Nov. 1977, 73).

Shortly before I began teaching early morning seminary in the fall of 1983, I checked back on the attendance records of the previous year. I was shocked to see that the twenty-five juniors and seniors that I would be teaching had 257 combined absences and 249 tardies (under-reported?) for the year. Even this really concerned me, even if the class did start at 5:55 A.M. I kept thinking about getting up that early and giving lessons to a handful of students while most of the class members were home asleep or late arriving.

My brother Jack was teaching the combined freshmen/sophomore class that year, so we discussed the problem and what we might do about it. This statement helped us put together a plan of action: "People respond to challenges; they don't respond to begging."

We decided to challenge each other's class to an attendance contest for the year. The class that had the most absences and tardies would fix a big breakfast for the winning class on the last morning of seminary.

When everyone arrived the first day (the only day they all normally come), I told the students that I had challenged the younger class to an attendance contest in their behalf. However, the challenge would not really be against others but only against themselves.

J.J., a senior, said, "What did you do that for?" I told him that I knew my class would enjoy challenges. Someone else asked what would happen if our class lost. I told them they would have to cook breakfast for the other class on the last day of seminary. Letitia turned to the class and said, "What do ya'll want to fix them on the last day?" Someone said, "Let's just bring them cereal. That's all they deserve."

Clearly, my class wasn't really into this challenge business. However, I wasn't going to cave in that easily. I had made a list of each student's attendance for the previous year and ranked them from the best to the poorest attenders. Veronica had the best attendance record. She didn't have any absences and only one tardy for the year. After the class settled down a little, I asked Veronica why she had been late for seminary once the year before. She said that the car she was driving had a flat tire. She ran home and switched cars, arriving a few minutes late for seminary.

I said with a smile, "Excuses, excuses. You should have

been better prepared." I could tell she got a little fired up by my statement, which was exactly what I wanted. I then said, "Veronica, I want to challenge you personally to an attendance contest. Me against you. No absences and no tardies for the year." Oh course, she quickly accepted my challenge. I then went to the next best attender and asked if he wanted to join us. He accepted.

Continuing down the list, I personally challenged each student to join in the competition. All accepted until we got to the bottom of the list. Those with the poorest attendance the previous year were very reluctant to accept the challenge. However, most of the students agreed to at least *try* to get 100 percent for the year.

Walking away that first day, I was really excited at first, and then it hit me what I had done. What if the electricity went off one time during the year, and I was late? What if I got sick? Veronica would beat me, and I would have to face the class. I didn't sleep well all year. I watched the clock most of the night to make sure I didn't sleep in. Of course, all of the twenty-five students did not achieve 100 percent attendance for the year, but we did make significant progress.

The next year I had a class of sixteen seniors. The first day of class all sixteen were in attendance. I asked them how they would like to set a national record.

"For what?" someone asked.

"For the best attendance at an early morning seminary class in history."

"What is the record?" someone else asked.

I told them I didn't have any idea but that I was absolutely positive that no one had ever exceeded 100 percent attendance at early morning seminary. I was surprised that everyone in the class agreed that it would be fun to try it.

One of the great days of my life was when the stake president announced at seminary graduation the next spring that the members of our class had achieved 100 percent attendance for the year. Not one student missed a single day that year. The class members bonded together in some remarkable ways.

Attendance Results

1982–83 257 Absences 249 Tardies

1983–84 49 Absences 71 Tardies

1984–85 0 Absences 42 Tardies

People do not respond well to begging, but they do respond to a challenge to strive for excellence. When we work hard in a worthwhile common cause, we grow closer together and receive blessings.

Following the counsel of the leaders of our great Church brings much happiness into our lives. I challenge you to read their teachings and look for ways to apply their counsel in your personal life.

Randal Wright was born and reared in Texas and currently serves as an institute of religion director for the Church Educational System. He holds a Ph.D. in Family Studies from BYU and has done extensive research on the impact of electronic media on adolescents. He has also written articles for several magazines and is the author of five books. He loves basketball, music, books, red velvet cake, and being at home with his family. He and his wife, Wendy, are the parents of five children and reside in Austin, Texas.